ESL Students in the Public Speaking Classroom: A Guide for Instructors

ESL Students in the Public Speaking Classroom: A Guide for Instructors

SECOND EDITION

ROBBIN D. CRABTREE
LOYOLA MARYMOUNT UNIVERSITY

DAVID ALAN SAPP
FAIRFIELD UNIVERSITY

with
ROBERT WEISSBERG
NEW MEXICO STATE UNIVERSITY

BEDFORD / ST. MARTIN'S
Boston ◆ New York

For Bedford/St. Martin's

Publisher for Communication: Erika Gutierrez
Developmental Editor: Julia Bartz
Publishing Services Coordinator: Lidia MacDonald-Carr
Production Associate: Victoria Anzalone
Marketing Manager: Tom Digiano
Editorial Assistant: Catherine Burgess
Project Management: Books By Design, Inc.
Copy Editor: Virginia Ruebens
Cover Design: William Boardman
Composition: Achorn International, Inc.
Printing and Binding: Edwards Brothers Malloy, Inc.

Manufactured in the United States of America.

9   8   7   6   5   4
f   e   d   c   b   a

For information, write: Bedford/St. Martin's, 75 Arlington Street, Boston, MA 02116   (617-399-4000)

ISBN 978-1-4576-5423-7

Preface

As American universities attract increasingly large numbers of culturally and linguistically diverse students, college instructors are becoming more aware of teaching challenges that arise from this growth in diversity. *ESL Students in the Public Speaking Classroom* directly addresses these challenges as they apply to the undergraduate public speaking course. It provides instructors with insights about the variety of non-native English-speaking students (including speakers of global English varieties), practical techniques that can be used to help these students succeed in their assignments, and ideas for leveraging this cultural asset for the education of all their students.

Orginally printed as a brief guide to supplement Bedford/St. Martin's public speaking textbook, *A Speaker's Guidebook*, this book has been expanded to meet instructors' increased desire for professional development in this area. Instructors who reviewed the original guide encouraged the idea, and Bedford/St. Martin's was interested in publishing our new text as part of the Bedford/St. Martin's Professional Resource series. With this opportunity, we were able to update and expand the book to include new conversations, focused chapters on technology and community engagement in public speaking courses, and an annotated bibliography for further reference.

This book is designed for instructors and graduate teaching assistants of undergraduate public speaking courses at colleges and universities that enroll international students and non-native English speakers from U.S. contexts. No special knowledge of linguistics or second-language teaching is necessary in order for instructors to benefit. However, we assume that readers have had some graduate course work in speech communication theory and practice and are familiar with the content of and current approaches to public speaking instruction.

This book can be seen as a professional resource to support the teaching of public speaking courses. It can be used in conjunction with Bedford/St. Martin's public speaking textbooks or as a reference tool for any college-level public speaking instructor whose classes include ESL students, speakers of global Englishes, and students with a variety of American dialects. We aim to assist instructors in seeing the linguistic and cultural diversity of their classes as an extraordinary teaching asset, and to guide instructors in using techniques that will help their students become more effective speakers within increasingly diverse rhetorical contexts.

APPROACH

ESL Students in the Public Speaking Classroom views public speaking from a cultural perspective: ESL and other linguistically diverse students are not seen as lacking preparation, but rather as possessing myriad cultural frames of reference that may influence their cognitive styles, language use, and learning behavior. We assume that linguistically diverse students are the intellectual equals of any other student in the public speaking classroom; some of them may, in fact, represent the educational elite of their home countries, and others may be among our most motivated and high-achieving students. Thus, the approach we have taken here toward teaching these students is additive, rather than remedial. That is, learning to do public speaking American-style is not a matter of replacing one set of behaviors with "better" ones, but rather a matter of all students acquiring greater cultural awareness and additional skills for making appropriate rhetorical choices in diverse speaking contexts. We encourage instructors to capitalize on the global perspective and cultural richness their students bring to class, and to take advantage of having linguistically and culturally diverse classes as a way to develop greater intercultural understanding and skill among all students.

SCOPE AND CONTENT

ESL Students in the Public Speaking Classroom consists of eight chapters dealing with cultural, pedagogical, linguistic, and rhetorical issues relevant to ESL students in public speaking courses. Chapters 1 and 2, using updated demographics that reflect the contemporary classroom, provide background information on the variety of linguistically diverse students college instructors are likely to encounter in their courses. These chapters also cover some of the cultural assumptions about classroom learning that students may bring with them. Throughout, the chapters provide ideas for improving all students' listening skills when interacting with various kinds of English speakers.

Chapter 3 covers common challenges in spoken English that are likely to contribute to ESL students' accents, along with suggestions for helping them overcome any speaking difficulties in pronunciation, vocabulary, and fluency that affect their comprehensibility and effectiveness. This chapter also offers new advice on how to encourage native English-speaking students to develop listening skills that help them interact effectively with their non-native speaking classmates. Chapters 4 through 6 offer planning, rehearsal, and feedback techniques designed to help ESL students deliver successful speeches. These chapters pay special attention to the rhetorical patterns employed by various cultural groups and offer suggestions for helping students from these groups meet expectations of a U.S.-based, native English-speaking audience. Expanded coverage includes a discussion on how ESL students can confront stereotypes and generalizations by recognizing and honoring their own cultural traditions.

The remaining content of the book is completely new to this edition:

- Chapter 7 focuses on ways that technology can support instruction, enhance students' speeches, and augment listening comprehension for all students in linguistically diverse classrooms. Some challenges and limits of technology are also introduced.

- Chapter 8 explores challenges and opportunities for community-engaged sections of the public speaking course given the growing prevalence of these approaches. While we provide some introductory material related to civic learning, service-learning pedagogy, and community engagement, the chapter emphasizes issues related to the needs of ESL students and the assets they bring to community engagement associated with the public speaking course.
- An annotated bibliography is provided for those interested in further reading. These sources may also be useful in developing additional course assignments to inform action research from your classroom context.

Throughout the book, new activities and assignment ideas are shared to help instructors leverage the assets of a culturally and linguistically diverse classroom and to support the development of speaking effectiveness among linguistically diverse students.

PRINT AND DIGITAL OPTIONS

ESL Students in the Public Speaking Classroom is available as a traditional print text as well as in a number of e-book formats that can be read online or downloaded to a laptop or tablet. Available versions include the Bedford e-Book to Go, Kindle, CourseSmart, Nook Study, Kno, and more.

ACKNOWLEDGMENTS

We thank the students and faculty who have inspired us in this work. This includes our undergraduate and graduate students and our colleagues at New Mexico State University, Fairfield University, Universidade do Sul de Santa Catarina, DePauw University, Universidad Centroamericana de Managua, University of Minnesota, Chattanooga State Community College, Saint Petersburg State University of Economics and Finance, University of Tennessee at Chattanooga, and China Agricultural Engineering University.

We also thank the many people at Bedford/St. Martin's involved in this book's publication, including Denise Wydra, Vice President for Humanities; Erika Gutierrez, Publisher for Communication; Julia Bartz, Senior Editor; Catherine Burgess, Editorial Assistant; the production team headed by Elise Kaiser, Lidia MacDonald-Carr, and Victoria Anzalone; and our marketing manager, Thomas Digiano. We appreciate comments by the reviewers of the original guide, whose feedback was helpful as we planned our revision: Raymond Bell, Calhoun Community College; Susan Cain, Southwestern Community College; Diana Cooley, Lone Star College; Douglas Hoehn, Bergen Community College; Joshua Galligan, Virginia Commonwealth University; Holly Roberts Mallory, Sullivan University; Laura Hudson Pollum, Concordia University – Chicago; and Lauren Teal, Grand Rapids Community College.

We hope *ESL Students in the Public Speaking Classroom* proves useful to you as you begin to work with your students. Based on our own experiences with linguistically diverse students, we anticipate that you too will find them to be among the most academically competent and motivated in your classes, and that they will enrich the learning experience for all. Helping them realize their potential as public speakers in English can be a truly rewarding experience.

Robbin D. Crabtree
David Alan Sapp
with
Robert Weissberg

About the Authors

Robbin D. Crabtree received her M.A. and Ph.D. in speech communication from the University of Minnesota. She is Dean of the Bellarmine College of Liberal Arts at Loyola Marymount University. She has also served on the faculties of DePauw University, New Mexico State University, Fairfield University, the Universidade do Sul de Santa Catarina in Brazil, and St. Louis University in Madrid, Spain. Dr. Crabtree has taught courses in public speaking and international, intercultural, and development communication since 1984. She has conducted research in Nicaragua, El Salvador, Cuba, India, Kenya, Brazil, Spain, and along the U.S.-Mexico border, with a particular interest in participatory and action research methods. Her work has been published in several national and international journals.

David Alan Sapp earned his Ph.D. in rhetoric from New Mexico State University. He is Professor of English at Fairfield University in Connecticut, where he serves as Associate Vice President of Academic Affairs. He previously taught at Chattanooga State Community College, University of Tennessee at Chattanooga, China Agricultural Engineering University, and Universidad Centroamericana de Managua. Dr. Sapp is a workplace communication specialist and currently serves as associate editor of the journal *Rhetoric, Professional Communication, and Globalization*. In addition to studying challenges in international technical and business communication, his research has focused on issues such as academic honesty, teaching challenges in online courses, and pedagogical theory and practice.

Robert Weissberg holds an M.A. in TESOL from UCLA and a Ph.D. in curriculum and instruction from New Mexico State University. He served as college associate professor in the communication studies department at NMSU and director of the International Intensive English Program. He has over 25 years of experience in teaching ESL in the United States, Central and Southeast Asia, and Latin America. Before his retirement, he taught courses in academic writing and speaking for non-native speakers and pedagogical grammar for ESL teachers in training; he also conducted training for NMSU's international graduate teaching assistants.

Contents

ESL Students in the Public Speaking Classroom: A Guide for Instructors

1

Linguistic Diversity in Today's Public Speaking Classroom

As the U.S. population becomes more diverse, instructors who teach public speaking at all types of postsecondary institutions can expect to see more students in their classrooms who are non-native English speakers. The International Institute of Education reports that there are now more than 825,000 international students enrolled in U.S. colleges and universities; this represents an increase of approximately 30 percent over the past fifteen years, despite the drop in international student enrollments that occurred during the years following the 9/11 attacks. Undergraduate and graduate student populations from China, India, South Korea, and Saudi Arabia now account for over 50 percent of the total population of international students. Increasing numbers of students from Indonesia, Brazil, Myanmar, Syria, and Ethiopia are the result of new intergovernmental partnerships or well-documented crises. This array of international students includes non-native English speakers, speakers of global Englishes for whom it may be a co-primary language, and immigrant students for whom English may be a second or third language.

Many of these international students, as well as students from linguistic minority populations in the United States, enroll in undergraduate public speaking classes, and their increasing numbers may at first glance seem to represent a serious instructional problem. How can these students—whose command of spoken and written English varies tremendously—be expected to prepare and present speeches that will hold the attention of their audience, let alone approach the quality of those of native speakers of English? Instructors of public speaking need to learn about and develop teaching practices that support students who struggle with aspects of academic and professional English.

Although English as a Second Language (ESL) students do pose a challenge to instructors, their presence in the speech class provides potentially far more benefits than obstacles. For that reason, we encourage instructors to welcome these students enthusiastically into their classrooms and to discourage their academic programs from isolating ESL students into dedicated sections of public speaking. International students and U.S. linguistic minorities represent a cultural, experiential, and linguistic resource that can enhance the public speaking experience for all students. This is not to say that instructors who encounter ESL students in their speech classes are not in for some extra work. It is indeed a tall order to teach public speaking of sufficient sophistication to students from non-English-speaking countries like China, Russia, and Brazil.

This book surveys some of the areas in which ESL speakers and other non-native speakers of standard American English (NNSSAE) may need specific types of help that are unique to these student populations, along with suggestions for how that help can be made available. We describe how instructors can benefit from the presence in their speech classes of ESL students, as well as students who speak localized and nativized varieties of English (e.g., those from India, Jamaica, and Nigeria). These students will undoubtedly bring useful insights in their roles as speakers and as listeners. These insights will in turn inform and support a robust environment where all students will learn to analyze and produce rhetorical acts for our increasingly complex and interdependent global context.

THE ESL COLLEGE STUDENT

We begin by looking at the characteristics of the prototypical ESL learner in the context of the public speaking class. The first thing we find, however, is that there is no such thing as a prototypical ESL learner. In fact, English is a truly global language, and most communication in English is now from a non-native English speaker to another non-native English speaker in a non-English-speaking cultural context. This reality makes the top priority the negotiation of clear and comprehensible communication, not precise adherence to rules. As communication teachers and scholars, we know that variant or imperfect English can still be highly proficient, and that ESL students are often as different from one another linguistically, academically, and culturally as they are from their native English-speaking U.S. classmates. Some of the important distinctions are presented in the following pages.

International Students

International students most likely had to submit a minimum score on the Test of English as a Foreign Language (TOEFL) to be admitted to a United States college. They were granted a student visa by the U.S. Immigration and Naturalization Service that allows them to stay in the country for the purpose of attending college. International students must have a fairly well developed knowledge of English in order to get over the TOEFL hurdle; that means they have usually studied English grammar extensively in their own countries, often from primary school forward, and that they are able to read well and have sizable English vocabularies. It does not always mean, however, that they speak English fluently or have advanced skills in listening comprehension. It is often the case, especially with students from Asian countries, that their knowledge of English grammar and writing is far better developed than their speaking, while for students from Middle Eastern countries, the opposite is often true. In another common variation, students coming from Nigeria, India, or other former British colonies are likely to have attended English-medium schools since high school and to have developed a great deal of fluency in both written and spoken English. With that said, the vocabularies, accents, and communication norms we describe for these NNSSAE can vary widely from those that predominate on your campus.

What the speech instructor needs to keep in mind, then, is that international students' initial lack of speaking ability does not mean that they do not know English. What it does mean is that it will take a little time for them to activate the linguistic knowledge that they have gained from years of study. As we will see, the public speaking classroom can be an ideal environment for this to occur. It will also be necessary for them to adapt their language abilities to the classroom audience, which also likely includes students from many different academic majors, many parts of the United States, and different age cohorts. It would not be uncommon for a majority of students in a public speaking classroom to have little prior experience interacting with native speakers of languages other than English.

International students are more often than not strong students—highly motivated, intellectually sophisticated, and self-disciplined. Many international students represent the educational elite of their home countries, coming from middle-class, upper-middle-class, and sometimes wealthy families who may have sent them to the best primary and secondary schools available. This is often the case because few U.S. postsecondary institutions provide significant financial aid to international students for undergraduate study. They are often risk takers who are not satisfied with the conventional educational experiences available at home and are willing to throw themselves into a strange culture and an uncomfortable language to achieve their personal objectives.

U.S. Linguistic Minorities

The other large group of non-native English speakers in American colleges and universities is made up of linguistic minority (LM) populations—students who are U.S. residents but who speak a language other than English at home. These students tend to be either immigrants or the children of immigrants. Their skill levels in English and their educational backgrounds may vary tremendously, and sometimes can be in strong contrast to those of the majority of international students. Some have lived in the United States for several years; many have attended American high schools, have jobs in the local area, and are firmly integrated into the life of the community.

Linguistic minorities may have English conversation skills approximating those of native speakers, and because they are more closely linked to U.S. culture, they are often more comfortable and fluent in verbal give-and-take than are international students. However, this ease of expression may be restricted to the social arena. Linguistic minorities' "school English" may be much weaker, a fact that often shows up in their academic writing. Their class papers may show weak grammatical control, and their academic vocabularies may be poorly developed. This is because many immigrant students learned their native language from birth through a good part of their early schooling and then learned English as a second language during later schooling; their educational development of advanced fluency and literacy in both languages may have been disrupted by migration though they still may be highly functional in both languages. This was our experience teaching many Mexican immigrants in the U.S.–Mexico borderlands region. Thus, for many linguistic minorities, their command of English proficiency is the mirror image of the international students': They may appear upon first meeting to have more language competence than they actually do.

Educationally, many linguistic minorities also stand in contrast to international students. Their academic skills may be more like those of their American peers, lacking the drive and self-discipline that many international students exhibit. Additionally, they may have gone to less prestigious schools and may not have strongly developed literacy skills in their first language.

Of course, it would be unfair to render instant judgments on the linguistic minorities and international students in your classes solely on the profiles sketched here. The most educationally disadvantaged students can be among our most driven and high achieving, and the most advantaged can be among those least able or engaged. Thus, it is vital to always remember that not all ESL students are alike, and that the students in any particular cohort of ESL or NNSSAE students can vary greatly. We simply note the importance of understanding some distinctions between two different types of ESL students who bring different strengths and weaknesses to the challenges of public speaking, and who thus may require different kinds of instructional support. At the end of this chapter, we will discuss some ways for speech instructors to get below the surface of their individual students' language abilities and find out more about their backgrounds and academic preparation.

Exchange Students

Exchange students are international students who are in the United States for a short period of time and who are not typically seeking a degree from a U.S. institution. They are often allowed great flexibility in registering for classes (e.g., waiving prerequisites) and may take only those courses in which they are interested. A strong desire to improve their English language skills may be one of their major reasons for participating in an international exchange program. If these students are placed with host families in the community, or integrated productively within the residence halls, they may become very socially active.

Exchange students who register for a public speaking class are not likely to do so because of college or departmental requirements, but rather out of a genuine desire to improve their skill in spoken English, in making oral presentations, or both. Some may be seeking a primarily social and practical immersion experience and may spend little time on coursework. Some exchange students take classes on a more ad hoc basis, such as au pairs working in the United States whose host families are required to pay for some courses. These students often audit courses, something difficult to accommodate in a public speaking class that requires so much participation. Instructors generally have the choice whether or not to admit auditors into their courses.

The number of exchange students in the United States is very small compared with the total population of international students described above; around 5 percent of international students are exchange students. Nevertheless, it is worth keeping some of the differences in mind, as these may affect motivations to learn course content.

LEARNING STYLES

Visual versus Auditory Learners

Just as socioeconomic status and linguistic and educational background distinguish ESL students from one another, so too do their styles of acquiring knowledge. Like many other students, some ESL students learn best when instructional materials are presented visually. This is particularly true for international students whose listening comprehension skills are low. These students will perform better when the instructor makes generous use of visual media such as PowerPoint slides and handouts. These aids will help ESL learners overcome the substantial difficulty of listening in a second or third language and taking notes at the same time. Other ESL students, particularly linguistic minorities who have been in the country for an extended period of time, will be able to rely more on their auditory comprehension for taking class notes.

To support more visually oriented students, instructions for graded speeches should be clearly spelled out in a handout or other written document. It is critical that all students be provided with a copy of the course syllabus, with all requirements clearly delineated, and a calendar outlining dates for speeches and other class activities. It is important to remember when designing these documents that they will be used by students with a variety of English abilities.

Memorizers versus Problem Solvers

International students from some parts of the world have been trained since their earliest school experiences to learn by means of rote memorization. Developing critical thinking and problem-solving skills is not stressed in all educational systems. This applies particularly to students from some Asian and Middle Eastern countries. On exams, students from these cultures have been trained to repeat back enormous quantities of material that they have read and memorized. They tend to score well on exams covering a finite body of printed material. However, they may have more difficulty with tasks that require them to apply information learned in class or from the textbook to solving practical problems, such as preparing a specific type of presentation on a topic of their own, or collaborating on a group project. Handouts specifying the steps needed to complete multistep assignments and recorded or live models of certain types of speeches can help these ESL students gain a better notion of what is expected of them.

Acquirers versus Non-Acquirers

By the time they reach college age, some ESL learners have acquired about as much English as they ever will. They have reached a level of personal comfort with their communication ability and do not feel a need to further refine their written or spoken language. This can be frustrating for instructors who attempt to help them reflect upon and revise their speech habits, especially in the area of pronunciation, one of the earliest features of the language to be acquired by learners. These students may seem oblivious or even resistant to the instructor's suggestions for change. The language of these speakers has "fossilized" (i.e., become resistant to change) because they have used English for so long that their pronunciation and grammar patterns are unconscious and automatic, just as is the case with a speaker's first language. This is often true of U.S. residents who have lived in the country for many years.

It is very important for instructors to keep in mind that these students are not necessarily being recalcitrant or uncooperative. Their language-learning mechanism has simply ceased to function actively. A lot of effort can be wasted trying to get such students to eliminate their accents. However, if accent functions as a barrier to effective communication, appropriate tutoring can help in areas in which improvements can be made. We will look at these issues in more detail in Chapter 3.

In contrast, other ESL speakers in the public speaking class may still be actively acquiring English. These students are still in the middle of the "learning curve," constantly adjusting their grammar, checking and refining their pronunciation, and learning new words. They are open to speech correction from the instructor and are continually absorbing new language forms from their surroundings and in daily interactions. An interactive environment like the public speaking classroom can be a highly effective language laboratory for such students, and the instructor may see significant improvement in the accuracy and fluency of their English over the weeks of the course.

These differences in acquisition style among ESL learners may be a function of the students' age, the strength of their motivation to learn, or even innate ability; they are less likely a result of willfulness on a student's part. As with any other skill or knowledge area, some people simply learn a second language more quickly, easily, and completely than do others. The authors of this book also reflect this variety of orientation, "ear," and capacity for second-language acquisition.

Introverts versus Extroverts

Another possible explanation for differences in the language-learning curve is ESL students' social style. One student may sit in the back of the class, rarely asking a question, participating in a discussion, chatting with classmates, or making eye contact, while another plunges in readily without fear or self-consciousness. These behaviors may be based less on the students' actual proficiency in English and more on other factors, including their own perceptions of their language ability, their level of comfort with the informal atmosphere of the American classroom, or their personality type. A student who has a strong grasp of English but who feels out of place in the sociolinguistic setting of the classroom may be outperformed by an average learner with strong self-esteem and a confident interaction style. These differences may also be due to culturally different assumptions about the "proper behavior" of teacher and students in a classroom (see Chapter 2). Or introversion may simply be a matter of personality, unrelated to the student's degree of proficiency in English or the culture of origin.

Whatever the specific cause of their reticence, introverted non-native speakers of English can be at a serious disadvantage in the American classroom, especially in speech classes, where a premium is placed on active participation and personal projection. Introverted ESL students can gradually learn to adjust to these expectations by participating in one-on-one and small-group exercises, however. There are two important ways in which these kinds of activities can work to the ESL student's advantage. First, they create opportunities for conversation practice, which introverted students may be lacking. Second, practice with peers can lessen the anxiety many ESL students may feel about standing in front of a group of strangers speaking a language in which they are not yet comfortable. These activities thus provide a bridge from the anonymity of the formal lecture-style class to the high involvement of the public speaking course and its assignments.

ACCOMMODATING THE NEEDS OF ESL STUDENTS IN THE SPEECH CLASS

It is not necessary to radically restructure the public speaking class because of the presence of one or two (or more) non-native English speakers. This would not be in the best interests of the ESL learners, who need to become accustomed to the realities of the American university classroom to support their holistic academic achievement. However, some simple accommodations can be made that will increase ESL students' chances of performing well on their speeches and other assignments.

Using Media and Technology

As mentioned earlier, it is important to provide visual backup to information given orally to the class. A syllabus with clearly identified due dates for speaking and writing assignments is essential. Additional descriptive handouts provided in advance of each assigned speech are also helpful. Making available recorded samples of upcoming speech assignments can give international students a gestalt for types of speech events and styles of speaking with which they may be unfamiliar. These practices also will support learning for first-generation college students, those from under-resourced secondary schools, students from historically underrepresented groups, those with learning disabilities, and probably most students. The point here is that the effort you put into supporting the learning of your ESL students will pay dividends for all students, as is the case with most effective and high-impact pedagogical practices.

Lecture Style

American university lectures can be difficult for international students to follow, due both to comprehension difficulties and to the fact that many U.S. instructors sprinkle their presentations with idiomatic expressions, remarks, and jokes comprehensible only to cultural "insiders," along with anecdotes, asides, and sometimes lengthy digressions. None of these features need to be eliminated; again, they are part of the U.S. university experience to which ESL students need to adjust. However, instructors should be aware of when and how frequently they employ these lecture features, since they all serve to increase listening difficulty for many ESL students.

Some of the listening load can be lightened if the overall organization of the lecture revolves around a few key points. These key points should be clearly highlighted through the use of explicit discourse signals (e.g., "OK, let's go on to the next main point") and visual reinforcement (e.g., PowerPoint slides). Other, more purely linguistic factors can influence the ESL students' comprehension of lecture material. These include an instructor's rapid speech rate and informal pronunciation (e.g., "Didja?" for "Did you?"), as well as unfamiliar or difficult concepts and poorly understood technical vocabulary.

Observing ESL students' nonverbal behavior during the lecture can alert the instructor to comprehension problems resulting from these features of language. If the instructor senses noncomprehension on the part of the ESL student(s), he or she can take a number of steps: (1) Ask the class directly if the point is clear, giving students the opportunity to ask for clarification; (2) Repeat or paraphrase a difficult concept; or (3) Illustrate a point with an example.

Chapter study guides for student use (distributed either before, during, or after the lecture) are time-consuming to prepare but are enormously helpful as a study aid, not just for ESL students but for the native English speakers in the class as well. An interactive study guide, where some information is left for the student to supply, is even more useful.

Class Discussion

Some ESL students may shrink into the woodwork during class discussions. This is natural for international students unfamiliar with the linguistic and cultural rules of the American college classroom; however, the instructor should not tacitly encourage such behavior by ignoring these students. The class will not benefit from having a few isolated outsiders hovering on the fringes of the give-and-take, and these students will have extremely valuable perspectives to share. While at first ESL students may prefer not to contribute to the discussion voluntarily, a few judicious questions or requests for comments directed toward them may help to bring them into the fold and encourage them to speak up as the semester progresses.

In inviting comments from or asking questions of ESL students, the instructor may need to allow them a longer than normal time to respond. Student rejoinders normally follow the instructor's initiating remark by one second or less; some ESL speakers, on the other hand, may require three seconds or more to process the instructor's comment or question and formulate a reply. The instructor as well as the rest of the class must have *patience* and *empathy*. Keep in mind that the additional time is not a result of the ESL student's being intellectually slow or linguistically incompetent, but rather is due to the student's having to do so much more cognitive work than the others in the class just to keep up with the material. Imagine yourself taking a content course taught completely in a language other than English, and you will have an idea of the enormous cognitive load with which many ESL students struggle.

Small-Group Work

As we all know, being a truly effective instructor takes a lot of work. If our students are from a variety of linguistic and cultural backgrounds, being effective requires even more effort. It need not fall completely on the instructor's shoulders. In fact, through the use of student group collaboration, much of the content of this book can be covered by the students in their own exchanges. You just need to guide them a bit. Be sure, however, to discuss the nature of group collaboration and your expectations for collaborative work with your students. As discussed in Chapter 2, ESL students, who may find collaborative work novel, may not understand that there are limits to collaboration.

Try to build student groups strategically, so that each group is diverse. This can be difficult since students are likely to congregate according to perceived similarity. If all the linguistic minorities, or all the athletes, or all the international students are in the same groups, this process is really of little benefit to the class. In diverse groups, with a series of useful discussion questions, students can come to understand from each other a variety of rhetorical traditions and how they vary. Students can guide each other's speech topics and organizational development through brainstorming activities and peer feedback on outlines. If they practice their speeches for each other as well, it may help them develop effective linguistic and persuasive strategies.

Two risks are run, however, in forming diverse groups. First, international students may feel so uncomfortable in their groups that they participate little, if at all. When it comes time to prepare a group assignment, the U.S. students may feel that they are "carrying" the ESL students. On the other hand, diligent international students may be taken advantage of by other members of the group and given more than their fair share of the workload. The international student may feel that this is a requirement for group acceptance or simply may not know how to refuse a task in a socially acceptable way. To minimize these risks, instructors would do well to monitor groups to ensure they are functioning for the mutual benefit of all members. This is an important practice whether or not your class and its groups are highly diverse.

Office Hours

International students may not be familiar with the concept of scheduled office hours. They may feel embarrassed or ashamed to approach the instructor privately; conversely, they may think that the instructor's door is always open to them. These are the consequences of being "new in town" and of contrasting cultural expectations the students may have. It is therefore up to the instructor to make the first move by inviting ESL students to drop by the office to discuss any questions or problems they may be having with the class sessions or assignments. Occasional one-on-one conferencing throughout the course may give ESL students just the boost they need to succeed (Chapter 5 presents some specific suggestions for these conferences).

We often use required office hours early in each term. This breaks the ice for all students and often results in much more student engagement throughout the term. This practice also avoids the pitfall of assuming ESL students (or any group of students) need extra help or of unnecessarily drawing attention to cultural and linguistic differences in ways students might find alienating.

Initial Language Assessment

An initial office visit early in the course is an excellent opportunity for the instructor to do an informal language assessment of each ESL student in the class. A relaxed conversation away from the stress of the classroom will provide an indication of students' actual listening and speaking levels. The instructor might even ask each student to write a brief description of previous public speaking experiences they have had. Some may be managers or teachers in their own countries with substantial public speaking experience. This writing task provides useful information, not only about students' backgrounds, but also about aspects of their English language knowledge that may not be apparent from their conversational speech. Most important, the assessment will give you an idea of how much (if any) additional support individual ESL students are likely to require to make it through the course successfully.

CONCLUSION

In the following chapters, we discuss in depth specific issues ESL learners, their instructors, and their classmates will face in the public speaking class. First, we look at some of the culturally determined assumptions and expectations that international students and other linguistic minorities bring to the classroom that are at variance with the conventions found in most U.S. colleges and universities. In Chapter 3, we look at some of the specific language difficulties that ESL students experience in speaking English and how to facilitate improvement. In Chapters 4 through 6, we explore issues specifically related to the planning, practicing, and presentation of speeches. Chapter 7 offers in-depth exploration of technology issues, both how instructor use of technology can support an optimal learning environment for ESL students and also how students might use technology in their speeches effectively to mitigate linguistic challenges. Chapter 8 addresses those faculty who use community-engaged pedagogies such as service learning or community-based research as the basis for speech assignments. It explores special challenges and opportunities for ESL, linguistic minority, and other students and offers suggestions for how to structure community-engaged courses and assignments. Throughout this book we ask speech instructors to bear in mind that while ESL learners can achieve as much as or more than their native English-speaking classmates, they may require more time, patience, and support in order to do so.

We close this chapter with a broad caveat about the cultural categories we engage throughout this book. As many scholars and teachers in communication studies and its related fields are aware, there are a variety of paradigms that frame our philosophical, theoretical, and empirical traditions. The social-scientific/positivist approach, for example, treats culture as a fixed variable largely associated with national contexts or demographic categories. The interpretive approach focuses on ethnographically derived and largely descriptive research of specific instantiations of cultural communication and/or intercultural contact. The critical/cultural approach, by contrast, examines culture as a site of contested identities and performances that are shaped and constrained by power dynamics within and across cultural groups in particular historical contexts. We find value in all of these approaches and try to keep them in mind, perhaps somewhat in dialogue with each other, throughout this book.

While we have tried to qualify any generalizations about students' cultural identities or their linguistic sensibilities, our treatment of the instructional context and its cultural and linguistic challenges is in fairly broad strokes. We invite readers to bring a dialogic perspective to the teaching challenges in culturally and linguistically diverse classrooms and to consider a variety of theories that might inform the work. Overall, our goal is to empower all students as learners: to raise consciousness about the ways culture influences the rhetorical situation, to value each other's and their own identities without fixing or "freezing" essentialized notions of collective cultures and individual identities, and to produce speech acts that advance their civic engagement along with their ability to succeed as communicators in contemporary global contexts.

CLASSROOM ACTIVITIES

Discuss with students how English is used in the world. Remind them that more people speak English as their second (or third) language than speak it as their first language. Ask them to provide reflections on these facts.

Discuss localized and nativized Englishes (e.g., varieties spoken in India, Jamaica, and Nigeria). Ask students to provide examples from their own families, friends, and travel experiences.

Discuss the terminology with the students: English as a Second Language (ESL), Non-Native Speakers of Standard American English (NNSSAE), and Linguistic Minorities (LM). Discussion could also include exploration of terms such as *foreign*, *international*, *exchange*, and *immigrant*. This discussion can help establish the range of students in the class and open the lines of communication about identity. It also can create an initial opportunity for students to discuss choice of words and audience analysis in their speeches.

CHAPTER

2

Cultural Assumptions, Variations, and Expectations

As in all contexts, people come to the educational context — the classroom — with a variety of expectations and assumptions. A classroom with the mix of students discussed in the previous chapter will likely be full of significantly mismatched notions about appropriate student conduct, the nature of peer relationships, and the respective roles of student and teacher. This chapter explores some of the cultural factors that influence these assumptions and expectations and suggests some ways you as the instructor can overcome potential problems, as well as harness this unique context for the benefit of all learners.

The chapter explains why students' expectations, attitudes, and behaviors may vary significantly in the classroom. Relying on the work of cultural and communication theorists and over sixty years of combined teaching experience in myriad domestic and international contexts, we offer empirical and theoretical frameworks along with anecdotes and examples that illustrate how cultural issues might manifest in the public speaking classroom and how instructors might both recognize and address them. The purpose of these suggestions is not merely to help you get your ESL and other linguistically diverse students to conform to conventional U.S. public speaking practices, though this may be of practical importance to some instructors. We hope, in addition, to guide you to help all students to understand (1) how expectations about classroom behavior and public speaking vary across cultures and (2) how a speaker can adapt speech content and style to the appropriate audience through recognizing the diversities that characterize most rhetorical situations. As a result, we hope that meaningful intercultural exchange will develop in the classroom where ESL and speakers of varied English dialects can often feel isolated or culturally marginalized.

EXPECTATIONS FOR TEACHERS

Since first walking into the university classroom as an instructor at the age of twenty-four, one of the authors knew that her age, gender, and California culture were somewhat foreign even to her native U.S. students in Minnesota. Many students were her age or older, and most had been born and raised in the Midwest. Her California slang was nonintelligible in some cases. For many of the students, her clothes, comportment, and discourse patterns seemed inconsistent with her position and expertise given common stereotypes about college professors.

The expectations for instructors held by many international students are likely to be quite close to these stereotypes. In many cultures, teachers are necessarily older than students, and in many countries few women have access to the education necessary to become university professors — particularly in traditional societies and developing countries. Nevertheless, students from a wide variety of cultures are increasingly coming to the United States for a university education, and we should be prepared to make our courses useful for and welcoming to them. At many universities, in fact, programs in business, engineering, and agriculture *require* their students to take public speaking as part of their general education (it is a popular general education *option* for liberal arts students) or as part of their training to be graduate teaching assistants, and these programs are drawing students extensively from Middle Eastern, sub-Saharan African, East Asian, and Latin American countries. While English may be an official, co-primary, or second language for students from many other cultures, the English dialects and accents of students from various parts of South Asia, Africa, the Pacific Rim, and Europe, along with a variety of related cultural and discursive norms, vary widely.

The diverse classroom provides an excellent opportunity to introduce culture as an object of study in the public speaking course. By making culture "problematic," instructors can heighten student awareness of the ways their own backgrounds and those of their classmates include a variety of similarities and differences that need to be considered as part of the rhetorical situation.

Instructors should look for opportunities to confront stereotypes when they come up in the classroom. It may be that many traditional-aged undergraduates raised in the United States may avoid verbalizing stereotypes — even if they employ them cognitively — due to their multicultural educational training in primary and secondary school and the ways the diversity movement in the United States has produced some fear of being seen as "politically incorrect." Interestingly, in our experience, our international students also may formulate and articulate stereotypes about themselves, perhaps because their own tacit cultural assumptions and unconscious norms are in sharper relief while studying in the United States. Thus, both voiced and unvoiced stereotypes arise in many classroom discussions, so there are ample opportunities to raise this issue.

All societies are diverse in multiple ways, and instructors can disrupt cultural stereotypes and generalizations through gentle reminders. One way is simply pausing the discussion in order to pose questions that invite student reflection on generalizations being made by a speaker or that might be operating in a class discussion. Students also can be encouraged to identify and question such generalizations when they are presented in speeches or discussions. The following cultural and communication issues should be kept in mind in a multicultural, multilingual public speaking classroom.

DIFFERENCES IN NONVERBAL COMMUNICATION

Norms for nonverbal behaviors generally and, in the classroom, specifically, vary tremendously across cultures. If teachers are not familiar with cross-cultural differences in nonverbal communication behaviors, they often misinterpret them. The ability to identify and understand these differences can be the single most important factor in building a successful learning environment for international students, and may also be consequential for other culturally diverse students as well.

Formality

One of the key variables is the relative formality of the classroom climate. With the growing popularity of participatory learning models in some disciplines, the U.S. classroom has become increasingly interactive and informal. This may be an awkward revelation for some international students. In Japan, for example, teachers are held in high regard, and students are expected to rise and bow to greet an entering teacher. By comparison, our classrooms may seem disorderly places where there is little respect for the authority of the teacher. Israeli students, on the other hand, may find our classes overly rigid and structured when compared with the noisy and spontaneous kibbutz classroom. It would be worthwhile to discuss cultural differences in classroom formality with your class and to invite international students to share descriptions and expectations of classrooms in their own cultures. Making the differences explicit is one way to delineate your own expectations to all the students, while also producing an opportunity for cultural exchange.

Time Orientation

Perhaps the most profound cultural difference is in *chronemics*, or time orientation. In the United States, where punctuality is valued and "time is money," we instructors tend to expect that students will arrive at class on time, manage classroom interaction with an awareness of the standard time-bank system (e.g., fifty-minute blocks, three times a week), and turn in assignments on schedule. International students may find this time orientation extremely alienating, believing that scheduled interactions are superficial and deadlines are negotiable based on personal circumstances. In Argentina, for example, it is not unusual for classes to begin up to forty-five minutes after the scheduled time, and even the professor may arrive this late without remark. Once class is under way, Argentine students may be willing to linger well past the scheduled end if the discussion is engaging. This stands in stark contrast to U.S. students, who typically watch the clock and begin stuffing notebooks into backpacks at precisely the moment class is over, whether or not the professor has wrapped up the lecture or ended the discussion.

The impact of differences in time orientation can be particularly significant in the public speaking classroom. In a fifteen-week semester (or worse yet, a ten-week quarter), scheduling speeches is an art. Students who arrive late or speak too long wreak havoc on the carefully planned syllabus. For example, a Korean student in one of the authors' classes felt no obligation to keep her speech within the five- to seven-minute allotment. For her, it was more important to relay the content to her classmates, as she explained later in response to the impact of timing on her grade. The instructor's attempts to balance the requirements of the course with culturally appropriate face-saving communication with the student were a challenge requiring cultural and interpersonal sensitivity. However, U.S. students may feel cheated if others (perhaps especially international and other linguistically diverse students) do not follow the assignment's time limitations or adhere to recognizable formats. Managing time is challenging for instructors in all classrooms; the public speaking teacher in a culturally and linguistically diverse classroom may find it to be one of the most significant challenges she or he faces.

Eye Behavior

Another nonverbal behavior that may produce misunderstandings is the cultural variability in *oculesics*, or eye contact and eye gaze. The dominant U.S. culture tends to value direct eye gaze and moderately sustained eye contact as signs of honesty, integrity, and engagement. For most native English speakers in the United States, it is a sign of attentiveness and respect to look at the teacher (or fellow student) when he or she is talking. Not doing so is often interpreted minimally as disinterest or, worse, as flagrant disregard. However, in some African and Latin American cultures as well as most American Indian cultures, an *averted* eye gaze can be preferred as the sign of attentive listening, and direct eye contact with a teacher might be seen as confrontational and disrespectful. One of the key points we teach about rhetorical ethos and public speaking delivery is the importance and impact of effective eye contact. Asking Apache or Blackfoot students, however, to make and sustain meaningful eye contact with audience members might cause them great distress or humiliation. It is easy to see, then, that teachers and students of different cultures could have monumental difficulties meeting each others' expectations for classroom interaction. As a result, this could have consequences for students whose speaking assignments are evaluated on the prevailing cultural norms rather than on their own. You should not take for granted that predominant norms will be known, understood, or easily adopted by all of your students.

Attire

How to dress for a classroom-based speaking assignment is another issue that should be discussed in relation to cultural norms, as well as to context-specific expectations. While many U.S. students may instinctively dress up for their formal presentations (e.g., interview attire), others are just as likely to show up in their everyday classroom attire, which tends to be quite informal, including t-shirts, jeans, sweatpants, and backwards baseball hats, all of which we have seen our students wear in classes where we have not articulated specific expectations. Many international students may find U.S. classroom dress habits comparatively informal, and may perceive them as wholly inappropriate for the classroom, even disrespectful to the instructor.

One way to approach this issue is to develop a set of clear parameters for presentation-day attire and communicate those parameters on your syllabus or with each assignment. It is worth giving students leeway to dress in a way appropriate to their topic rather than in a standardized way. You might ask your students to help develop what will be the class norms and expectations for attire on presentation days. Having students discuss normative attire for a variety of common contexts is a worthwhile exercise. Take the opportunity to point out cross-cultural variations, as well as to situate choice of attire in relation to audience analysis and speaker credibility.

Personal Space and Touch

Two other nonverbal communication norms that might affect classroom interaction are variations in *proxemics* and *haptics*, or the use of personal space and touch, respectively. It is widely known that people from the United States tend to require a good deal of personal space to feel comfortable. While we might consider two to three feet the minimal distance for casual social interaction, members of cultures considered "high contact" may expect much smaller distances in a normal interaction. In group activities, for instance, some international students can create a high level of discomfort for U.S. students by attempting to close the distance to one they find comfortable.

Similarly, appropriate norms for touch in the classroom vary. In these highly litigious times in the United States, virtually all forms of touch are discouraged in the educational setting, other than perhaps a professional handshake at the end of the semester. This could seem cold and alienating to some international students, who might expect to embrace their teacher in passing on campus or to receive reassuring or congratulatory hugs after a speech. Clearly, touch norms vary tremendously based on gender, both in terms of who touches whom and in terms of how touch is perceived depending on the sex of the person who touches and the one who is touched. While teaching in locations such as Brazil, China, and Nicaragua, we have often been surprised by the variations in these expectations among our students and fellow instructors.

As with most communication misunderstandings or mismatched expectations, we recommend a meta-communicative approach. Being sensitive to these and other variations in social interaction norms, talking openly about the differences within the class, and explicitly negotiating and voicing your classroom expectations are essential. Not only does this open the classroom to meaningful intercultural dialogue, but it clarifies many student and instructor expectations that are often mistakenly assumed to be understood and shared.

CULTURAL DIFFERENCES IN LEARNING AND COGNITIVE STYLES

Research has shown that culture has a significant influence on the ways students approach learning. Here we discuss some of the differences you may encounter, with particular attention to the ways these differences can manifest themselves in the public speaking course. Once you are aware of the variables discussed here, you'll be surprised to see how obvious some of these things become. Again, we contend that instructor awareness is a major step toward decreasing intercultural misunderstanding in the classroom and toward maximizing the learning opportunities the classroom offers.

Direct versus Indirect Communication

According to communication scholars, the relative directness of a culture's communication is one of the fundamental factors in understanding its values and patterns of social interaction. In so-called low-context cultures like the dominant white culture of the United States, verbal directness is valued, and important information is expected to be vocalized in most situations. In high-context cultures such as China, however, indirectness is more highly valued so that group harmony and interpersonal "face" can be maintained. In such cultures, important information goes unspoken, but is often understood within the context of social relations.

As you can imagine, these vastly different approaches to interaction can create misunderstandings and mismatched expectations in the public speaking classroom. As instructors, we may encourage open communication between students and ourselves and expect students to get to the point quickly in their speeches, as well as in office-hour chats. This expectation may not be easy to meet for some international students, whose natural and preferred mode of communication is more subtle and indirect. We will take this issue up again in Chapter 4 when we address helping linguistically and culturally diverse students plan their speeches.

Field Dependency and Independency

Another cultural variable that has been studied extensively is the degree to which students are field-dependent in their learning style. Field-independent learners enjoy abstract problem solving and can handle content that is highly theoretical — in other words, independent from context. In the United States, for example, especially in certain disciplines, field-independent learning dominates the educational system. American Indian and Mexican students, on the other hand, may come from more field-dependent educational backgrounds and may expect subject matter to be tightly related to practical problems and familiar contexts. Working to provide a variety of cultural examples for theories and concepts presented in lectures, as well as encouraging students to generate their own resonant examples, will help ESL and culturally diverse U.S. students grasp course material.

As an instructor, you should anticipate that field dependence/independence may also affect your students' choice of speech topics and organizational patterns. For example, American Indian students from traditional or reservation schools may be accustomed to learning by watching and might be more comfortable being assigned a demonstration speech. Of course, given that the privilege of speaking in public is highly limited and complex in American Indian cultures, even this solution is overly simplistic. You may need to consider these issues when designing your course and include assignment options with culturally diverse students in mind. Students can provide information about appropriate public speaking settings in their cultures and even propose alternative speech topics that would be more typical in their own cultures. In any event, you, as the instructor, should make it clear that the public speaking practices you are teaching are practices that will be most effective with audiences in a specific culture but may be unfamiliar and uncomfortable for your students from other cultures.

Tolerance of Ambiguity

One of the most prevalent theories of communication is uncertainty/anxiety management theory. Basically, this theory argues that new situations are filled with uncertainties that produce anxiety for people. Communication is the primary means by which we reduce uncertainty and, therefore, anxiety. This theory also argues that there are minimum and maximum anxiety thresholds. In situations that produce anxiety levels below the minimum threshold, we are likely to become bored. In situations where the maximum threshold of anxiety is exceeded, we may become psychologically distressed and communicationally dysfunctional. This theory may go a long way toward explaining and predicting dominant U.S. cultural communication practices, particularly between strangers in initial interactions.

Uncertainty may not produce similar reactions among all students. While U.S. students might prefer a highly predictable classroom environment (where the syllabus delineates activities for each class day, for example), others may expect and value spontaneity. Some cultures are more tolerant of ambiguity, uncertainty, and contradictions. If course materials, grading expectations, and interaction patterns are not clear or understood, U.S. students are likely to ask questions, whereas some international students may not feel the need to inquire about such uncertainties.

Similarly, our relative intolerance for ambiguity means that we tend to emphasize right/wrong and yes/no answers to questions. However, other cultures — for instance, those of India — do not see truth in such absolute terms and are not uncomfortable with ambiguity or contradiction. One of the authors' experiences in India reinforced these notions; she noticed that due to the numerous spoken languages and the plethora of local dialects, there was a high level of uncertainty in most interactions. Nevertheless, no one seemed upset by this uncertainty or by the countless misunderstandings that inevitably ensued.

The public speaking classroom produces a great deal of anxiety for most students. David Letterman once cited a study about people's greatest fears, which found that public speaking was number one, and death was number two. While many students will find the public speaking class to be anxiety-producing, this anxiety will vary greatly depending upon students' culture of origin and their status in that culture vis-à-vis public address, as well as their English-language ability. Assessing students' apprehension early in the semester may help you anticipate their levels of speech anxiety. Meeting with students to discuss their cultural assumptions, expectations about public speaking, and perception of their own linguistic challenges can help you understand the cultural meanings of and variety of reasons for speech anxiety.

Reflectivity/Impulsivity

We saw earlier how linguistic differences can affect ESL students' response time in class discussion and Q & A sessions. Culture also influences how long students will think about a question before answering it. In the United States, we tend to reward students who have the answer first, and students may compete by shooting their hands up quickly to get your attention. Even an incorrect answer may receive a favorable reply along the lines of, "Well, that's close, can you clarify a bit?" More recently, with the educational emphasis on student self-esteem and empowerment, as well as more dialogic pedagogies, an incorrect answer may even be explored for its relative merit as an alternative explanation or to stimulate student sharing of different perspectives and arguments. In other cultures, however, answering a question quickly but incorrectly may be a sign that one did not reflect long enough or was not thoughtful enough in forming one's response, which can result in a tremendous embarrassment or loss of face.

Furthermore, given the relative discomfort with prolonged silence in U.S. culture, a student's reflectivity may be interpreted as a sign she or he does not know the answer, and the instructor may move quickly on to someone else. Members of American Indian and Asian cultures, both of which are considered high-context, value prolonged silences and tend to be highly reflective in the classroom. This stands in stark contrast to some U.S. students, as well as students from some Middle Eastern cultures (e.g., Saudi Arabia, Israel) where open, intense, and confrontational-style debate is more normative. Instructors who are aware of the reflectivity/impulsivity variable can allow more time for students to answer questions, being sure to facilitate the discussion so that the ideas of many students are considered. You should be cautious about attributing passive communication to shyness, low learning ability, or even English proficiency, as discussed in Chapter 1. Rather, you should acknowledge the cultural appropriateness of these students' behaviors and provide encouragement and practical examples.

Academic Honesty and Integrity

Just as the nature of "truth" may be culturally variable, notions about what constitutes cheating vary extensively across cultures. In China, for instance, students report that they work hard to develop compensatory skills in order to succeed in a highly competitive educational environment. They often work in groups to help each other "beat the system"; ironically, cheating can be highly collaborative and cooperative there, and this behavior is not necessarily viewed as dishonest or unethical. Some international students report that they did not know certain activities were considered cheating. Two Saudi students in different sections of a public speaking course, for instance, worked on one speech together, and they each delivered it to their respective instructors, not understanding that this was unacceptable in the U.S. university setting. Another aspect of this example is the students' sense that speech *delivery*, not content preparation, was the most important skill to demonstrate in a public speaking course.

Similarly, instances of plagiarism should not be particularly surprising. In the individualistic culture of the United States, knowledge is copyrighted and individually owned. By contrast, in cultures with an oral tradition, knowledge tends to be thought of as collectively owned. Stories that are passed down from generation to generation as cultural knowledge may not be copyrighted or even authored. A student from such a culture might find it difficult to understand the practices of paraphrasing, attributing all ideas to their source, and referencing in APA style. You shouldn't take it for granted that all students have read the university's policy on plagiarism, or that they understand it when they do. One activity that we include in introductory courses is a library research session where our expectations of knowledge attribution are made explicit. In the age of online journals and Web-based research, this session benefits all the students and creates an opportunity to discuss varied cultural assumptions and practices.

CONCLUSION

This chapter has only grazed the surface of the kinds of issues that can arise in a culturally diverse public speaking classroom. While we have outlined some of the broad cultural concepts and how they may influence cultural variability in learning style, we should also provide a caveat. What we know about cultural differences in nonverbal behavior, cognitive style, learning style, and so forth are generalizations from previous ethnographic and social scientific research. Still, not all students from Eastern or American Indian cultures, or all native English speakers in the United States, or students from any other background will fit into neat behavioral categories. For instance, while Singapore is considered a high-context collectivistic culture, one student from that country belied every stereotype. She was verbally direct, even confrontational, and as individualistic as any of her U.S. counterparts. You should also note that the acculturation of your non–U.S. students is progressive; newcomers may be much more likely to adhere to their own cultural norms and expectations than will students who have been at the university for a year or two. U.S.-born and immigrant language minority students may manifest behaviors from both heritage and U.S.-dominant culture. Further, all students' choices may vary across contexts in order to demonstrate adaptation, on the one hand, or to assert a divergent cultural identity, on the other. Cultural norms along with performative choices and rhetorical aims may produce surprising variations that create opportunities for collective analysis and learning.

Finally, in teaching the basic principles of communication, you should be aware that most of our general communication theories and concepts are based on studies conducted in the so-called West and thus may not be applicable to people from other cultures. This can be uncomfortable for new instructors, who may not be prepared to discuss the relative merits of the material they have been assigned to teach. We recommend you adopt a nondefensive posture, allowing international students, linguistic minorities, and other students of non-dominant U.S. cultural backgrounds to present their divergent voices in a way that can enhance your instructional goals. This may expand your instructional horizons and student learning in exciting ways. Creating a space for culturally diverse viewpoints and experiences will enrich the learning environment for everyone, and this should be an important goal for public speaking classes today.

CLASSROOM ACTIVITIES

In dyads, have students share a fond memory of a classroom experience during their elementary school years. They should describe the teacher's interactions with students, the classroom, typical assignments and activities, and interactions with peers. Ask them to share a vivid example — one specific snapshot moment — to illustrate the essence of their prior academic experience. Then bring the class together and discuss how early childhood educational experiences shape our expectations for normative classroom behavior and dynamics. Point out any cultural variations that emerge in the examples and discussion.

Ask the class to generate a list of all the factors in the identity of speakers and audience members (e.g., race, class, gender, nationality, language, ability, etc.) that may influence speech topic, speech organization, speaking style, and audience reception. List these on the board — it will be a long list — in order to impress upon students the many features of public speaking that may be influenced by the audience and speaker's identity.

Have students briefly analyze in writing their current attire as to its appropriateness for a class presentation or public speech. Then ask volunteers to complete the following statement: "On my presentation day, I would not wear _____, because _____." The rest of the students can be invited to share exceptions to each student's rule: "You could wear your _____, if your speech was about _____." Or "You could wear your _____, if you wanted your audience to think/feel/believe _____."

Ask students to generate a list of attributes and behaviors that contribute to their personal and professional integrity, or ethos, as students who want to be perceived as trustworthy, honest, and credible. When issues such as "citing sources" come up, ask students to discuss whether there are cultural variations in how ethos is established, and affirm the expectations for academic honesty and integrity that are included in the syllabus.

Divide the class into small groups with some attention to making the groups diverse. Have each group discuss one of the nonverbal behaviors and share personal experiences that animate the points about cultural variations in communication behavior and norms. Have each group report to the whole class.

Ask each student to give a short "speech" without using verbal language or vocalizations, as in the game of charades. The instructor might demonstrate, miming a political stump-speech with exaggerated gestures and facial expressions, for example. This process will help students understand the importance of the nonverbal elements of public speaking. Take the opportunity to point out ways that nonverbal behaviors can support speech content and speaker credibility, as well as the ways nonverbal behaviors may detract from these.

Have students keep a "personal space" journal for one day. Ask them to record what they notice about how they, their friends, and others use personal space, with particular attention to situations where there are interpersonal interactions or group discussions (e.g., in line at the coffee shop, waiting at the bus stop). Take time in class to discuss what they noticed, and extrapolate the observations to a discussion of contextual and cultural differences that might influence public speaking situations.

3

Improving Comprehensibility of Speech

Non-native speakers of English, speakers of global English varieties, and U.S. linguistic minority students bring to the public speaking class a variety of linguistic factors that affect their ability to produce English that is comprehensible to others. In the first speech of the course, you will most likely become aware of problems that affect your ESL students' ability to communicate orally. Some of these problems will be related to *accuracy* (i.e., the speaker's control of the lexicon, sound system, and syntactic structures of English); others will affect *fluency* (the speaker's ability to produce a stream of speech smoothly and easily). Highly proficient ESL speakers demonstrate high levels of both and are thus able to make themselves comprehensible in public speaking situations despite having an accent from another place. Other non-native English-speaking students may have difficulty with aspects of either accuracy or fluency, or both, to the extent that their class presentations are compromised.

It is worth noting that similar issues may arise related to American regional dialects, the effects of bilingualism on speaking habits, or with global English variations. For example, accents and lexicon common in the American South may be quite unfamiliar to classmates from other parts of the United States. In the U.S.–Mexico border region where we taught for many years, there are differing attitudes among bilingual people about speaking with a Spanish accent; conversely, many native English speakers adopt speech patterns (pronunciation, cadence, etc.) similar to the spoken English of native Spanish speakers. Anyone who has ever turned on the subtitles of an Irish or New Zealand film is aware that native English is not the same everywhere. It may be of use to point out these types of issues so that all students come to better understand that spoken English varieties are common and to help disrupt ethnocentric linguistic attitudes that sadly are all too common in the United States.

In terms of focused work with non-native English-speaking students, it rests with the instructor to determine whether an ESL student's oral ability is problematic enough to fall into this category and whether it thus requires special assistance. The harder a student has to strain to understand what a speaker is saying, the more likely it is that oral skills fall below the threshold of acceptability. This will affect listening comprehensibility for the instructor as well as for the other students. In this chapter, we examine five aspects of oral language (four related to accuracy, one to fluency) that speech instructors need to be conscious of when ESL and other LM students are enrolled in their classes. While this book focuses on speaking, and this chapter focuses on the production of speech, various related factors related to listening comprehension of non-native English speakers and their speech audiences are mentioned, as well.

PRONUNCIATION

The most obvious element in a non-native speaker's accent is pronunciation. Nearly all the sounds that make up a non-native speaker's English pronunciation are approximate substitutions for the actual sounds used by native English speakers. These substitutions are rooted in the student's native-language sound system. Because languages vary tremendously in the specific sounds they make available for speakers to use and in the way those sounds are produced by the vocal organs, it's inevitable that virtually all ESL students' English pronunciation will be affected by an accent to some degree.

The question that concerns the public speaking instructor is as follows: Which specific features of their ESL students' pronunciation, if any, seriously interfere with their ability to make their speeches comprehensible? For students whose English has a high degree of phonetic accuracy, defined here as adherence to standard American pronunciation in the region where the course is taught, these features may be few or virtually nonexistent; the only effect of interference from these students' first-language sound system is to leave their English with a slight accent. For many speakers, this is a decided plus, since it gives their spoken English a unique and often appealing quality that may actually enhance their class presentations. In these cases, the best intervention is no intervention at all.

However, when there is more substantial interference from students' first-language sound system, their English pronunciation may be affected to the point that their comprehensibility is seriously degraded. In such a case, your first task is to determine which specific pronunciation features are contributing to the problem. These are sometimes difficult to pin down, but by listening closely to a video or an audio recording of the student's speech, you can begin to identify where the problems are. Fortunately, most of the sound substitutions that ESL students make follow consistent patterns; for example, a student may consistently substitute the /ee/ sound in *beat* for the /i/ sound in *is*, or /v/ for /w/, not just in one word but in a whole range of words. Once you have figured out what the patterns of substitution are, you can help students correct whole sets of mispronounced words by calling their attention to a few pertinent examples. You also should encourage native speakers of English to develop listening attitudes and skills that will support the comprehensibility of the non-native speakers. Communication is, after all, a shared responsibility, and it behooves all of our students to become more accustomed to interacting with speakers of global English varieties and native speakers of other languages, even if English is the lingua franca in many settings.

Vowels

In some cases, an English vowel is actually made up of two vowels tied together, like the /au/ sound in *about*. In fact, nearly all English vowels, even the apparently simple ones, are in reality complex sounds. Think of the minute vocal changes you have to make just to pronounce the simple word *oh*. If you say the word slowly, you can hear the little off-glide at the end made by the rounding of your lips. Or listen to the way the /a/ sound is made when you pronounce the word *radio*. The /a/ sound is off-glided into an /ee/, made by raising the middle of your tongue slightly at the end of the sound.

In contrast, many other languages use "pure" vowels, with little or no off-gliding. Spanish is a good example of this; think of the pronunciation of the /a/ and /o/ in a simple Spanish name like *Paco*. ESL students often import their own vowel sounds into English, substituting them for the standard English varieties. Generally, even with this variation, this has little serious effect on their comprehensibility.

In other cases, however, sound substitution can lead to misunderstanding. For example, if a student who is attempting to pronounce the word *kiss* instead produces something more like *keys*, the meaning of the sentence may be lost. The same thing happens when *hat* comes out sounding like *hot*. If you notice this to be a consistent pattern in a student's pronunciation, and one that interferes with comprehensibility, a private session with some focused work on one or two problem vowel sounds may be helpful. You can do this by drawing attention to a few example words from a student's recent speech that follow the mispronunciation pattern and by then having the student repeat the correct pronunciation after you. After the words have been pronounced accurately in isolation, have the student use them in phrases or complete sentences from the speech, maintaining the same level of accuracy.

Consonants

Consonant sound substitutions are easier to deal with than vowels because the way they are produced is often clearly visible to the observer, rather than hidden inside the speaker's mouth. Most challenges affecting pronunciation of consonants are the result either of substituting one articulation for another or of misusing aspiration or voicing.

Articulation. *Articulation* refers to the way the vocal organs come together (either at the lips, the teeth, or farther back in the mouth) to initiate sound. For example, some ESL students have difficulty differentiating the /sh/ sound from its close cousin /ch/. The difference is that the first one is made by pushing air over a small space between the tongue and the ridge behind the teeth, while the second is made by eliminating the space and actually touching the ridge with the tongue. ESL students whose first languages don't differentiate these two sounds may say *share* when they mean *chair* (or vice versa), or *shoes* when they mean *choose*.

The well-known /l/ vs. /r/ confusion of many Japanese speakers of English is another example of misarticulation. In fact, the English /r/ is notoriously difficult for many ESL students, regardless of their first language, and can seriously affect the comprehensibility of words in which it occurs. Pronounce the /r/ sound slowly yourself, and you'll notice that it is made by curling the tongue toward the back of the mouth and then flipping it forward in preparation for the next sound. The trick for non-native speakers is not to let the tongue come in contact with any part of the oral cavity until the next sound is made. Contrast this /r/, for example, with the Spanish /r/ pronounced more as /d/ or the trilling double /r/. Those English speakers who have studied Spanish and have struggled to produce those /r/ variations will empathize with the difficulties non-native English speakers may face.

It is up to you as the instructor to decide whether these consonant sounds are worth working on in a private session. If you think they warrant special attention, show students the correct point of articulation (describing it, if necessary) and have them pronounce a few example words slowly at first, then more quickly, finally using them in a phrase or a full sentence from their speech. Many universities have TESOL programs, ESL support services, and/or writing/speaking centers where students can access more focused support and practice.

As mentioned above, the sound substitutions ESL students use when speaking English are rooted in first-language habits established at a very early age and practiced intensively thereafter. It is consequently difficult for adult students to become aware of, let alone change, their patterns of pronunciation. It helps to let students know when certain mispronunciations seriously affect the quality of their speeches, others' comprehension and therefore the impact of their speech on the audience, and possibly even their grades; otherwise, they may not be sufficiently motivated to make the considerable effort required to adapt their phonetic habits.

Aspiration.   *Aspiration* is the little puff of air that accompanies some consonant sounds. Aspiration is one of the features that differentiate the sound /p/ from /b/ at the beginning of words, for example. Spanish speakers of English often fail to aspirate the /h/ sound at the beginning of words like *hotel*, which results in a pronunciation that sounds like *otel*. Southeast Asian and Middle Eastern speakers of English who don't aspirate the initial /p/ may not be able to pronounce the difference between words like *pair* and *bear*. One way to help students increase their level of aspiration is to have them hold a hand directly in front of their mouth and increase the level of aspiration until they can actually feel the puff of air against their open palm.

Voicing.   *Voicing* refers to the vibration of the vocal cords to produce sounds like /g/ and /v/ (as opposed to /k/ and /f/, which are made at the same points of articulation, respectively, but without vibration). It also explains the difference between sounds like /s/ and /z/ (this is another important difference in the pronunciation of *kiss* and *keys*). Students from language backgrounds that don't permit the voiced /z/ sound after a vowel will find it difficult to pronounce English words like *prize*; it will come out sounding more like *price*. Similarly,

Southeast Asian students may be unable to distinguish words that end in voiced consonants, like *bag*. The result will sound something like *back*.

If confusion related to voicing results in comprehensibility problems (a student referring to the *Nobel Price* may or may not be misunderstood), you can help students add voicing to their consonants. Have them hold one hand to their Adam's apple (or yours) while pronouncing a contrasting pair of words (*fault* vs. *vault*, for example). They can actually feel the vibration when the voiced sound is produced. Again, it's important to contextualize the practice for the student; pronouncing isolated sounds or words without incorporating them into meaningful phrases or sentences makes it unlikely that students will remember to transfer the corrected sound over to their speeches.

One final issue related to pronunciation concerns homonyms—words that have multiple meanings, or different words that share the same pronunciation. For example, *box* can be a container or a sport. *Merry, marry,* and *Mary* are pronounced in exactly the same way in some parts of the United States, while in other areas these words may vary in subtle ways. It is typical and appropriate for faculty to strictly enforce the correct use of *there, their,* and *they're* in students' written work. However, it can be a challenge for students to be aware of the use and pronunciation of homonyms in natural speech. Invite students to think consciously about their use of homonyms, the importance of context to understanding homonyms, and how homonyms may be distracting for non-native speakers of English.

SENTENCE AND WORD STRESS

Every language has its own cadence, or sound patterns, that might be likened to the melody of a song. Native speakers learn this cadence growing up through listening to and imitating the "melody" of their parents and others with whom they interact frequently. Cadence varies across languages, and non-native speakers usually bring their native language cadence to their spoken English. While this is associated with accent, it can best be understood through breaking it down into the companion characteristics of sentence stress and word stress.

Sentence Stress

One of the most characteristic features of spoken English is the tendency of native speakers to take one word in every sentence and give it a stronger push than the others. This feature is called *primary stress*. If you try out a couple of sample sentences, you'll notice that the primary stress normally falls at the end, or very close to the end, of the sentence.

"That was one of the best speeches I've ever heard!"

"Let me know if you have trouble, and I'll be glad to help you."

In the first example, the primary stress falls on *heard*; in the second, it falls on *trouble* and *help* (there are actually two sentences in the second example). In normal speech, we run the earlier words in the sentence together quickly, almost in a monotone, until we arrive at the emphasized word or syllable, which is pronounced not only louder than the others, but also with a higher pitch. This is critical to producing a comprehensible accent in English. Other languages have different stress rhythms, and like native-language vowel and consonant sounds, they are often carried over into English by speakers of other languages. To illustrate, imagine or listen to someone mimicking Yiddish- or Scandinavian-accented English, and you will notice that misplaced sentence stress plays a prominent role in the effectiveness of the impression.

If ESL students' speech delivery sounds choppy and disjointed, it is probably because they aren't using accurate sentence-stress patterns. When the problem is serious enough to affect comprehensibility, some focused practice may be helpful. Have the student write out a few sentences from the speech. Read the sentences aloud for the student, calling attention to the point of primary stress. Then ask the student to do the same. Then have the student read aloud several consecutive sentences from the speech, focusing on the overall stress rhythm. Finally, have the student repeat or paraphrase the sentences extemporaneously, without the text, maintaining the same stress pattern. Then monitor the student's delivery in class to see if the practice has transferred over to formal speech-giving. Students can use audio and video recordings to help them identify and adjust their speech habits.

Word Stress

Misplaced word stress can also diminish comprehensibility. Unfortunately, English word stress is less predictable than sentence stress. Take a two-syllable word like the verb *control*. Note that the final syllable is pronounced more strongly than the first. On the other hand, the word *crisis* has the opposite pattern. In polysyllabic words like *comfortable, embarrassing,* or *elementary,* the stress is even more variable. Since rules are of little help here, it is best to help the student make a list of a few troublesome words that seriously interfered with communication in a previous speech. As with sentence-stress problems, you should model each word first, with the student repeating. Then the student can work them into meaningful phrases and full sentences.

Sentence- and word-stress inaccuracies are difficult to change, and "over-learning" may be necessary to establish new habits. For extended practice, ask the student to have a native English speaker make a practice recording of all the words on the list and to practice them repeatedly. Native-speaking classmates who participate in such exercises might be asked to write up what they learn about language, their own and that of their partner, and how it supports the development of their own listening skills.

SYNTAX

Another aspect of language accuracy is the grammatical structures speakers use in forming phrases, clauses, and sentences. In speech, most syntax flies by so quickly that listeners are largely unaware of it. For example, if a non-native

English speaker says in a speech, "Is very complicated the social structure of my country," instead of "The social structure of my country is very complicated," some listeners will be totally unaware of the inverted phrases, while others may realize that there was something strange about the sentence but will have no trouble understanding it. However, there are a few critical syntactic errors that can result in loss of comprehension for the audience.

Pronouns

ESL students from a variety of first-language backgrounds, even fairly fluent ones, may fail to mark their pronouns consistently for number (singular/plural) or gender (masculine/feminine). That is, *he, she, it,* and *they* may be confused, as may *him, her,* and *them.* A possible reason is that English, unlike many other languages, is relatively indifferent to these functions in nouns (compared with Spanish or French, for example, where every noun — and adjective — is marked not only for number but also for gender). ESL students, assuming that these grammatical functions play a less important role in English, may be lulled into the expectation that they are simply not important. This is not true in the case of pronouns, however. If *he, she, it,* and *they* are constantly confused, serious miscommunication can result.

Further confusion results when subject pronouns are omitted altogether. This is permissible in many languages when the subject is already well established earlier in the discourse, but it's generally not the case in English. Because the subject slot in an English sentence is the "who or what I am talking about" part of the message, students who drop subject pronouns risk confusing or misleading their audiences.

Pronoun problems are more likely found in the speech of international students than in that of non-native U.S. residents. In either case, simply bringing these lapses to your students' attention is often sufficient to remedy the problem. They are probably aware of English pronoun rules academically but may not be aware that they are not applying them in their speech. They may need to hear a recording of one of their own speeches to realize that they are dropping or switching pronouns.

Verbs

Gender and number in English verbs are not an issue for ESL students (with the exception of the third person singular *-s* ending), but tense is. If a student uses a verb tense that isn't necessary — as in "When the manager *will see* this problem, he should correct it immediately" — the communicative effect is trivial and may go unnoticed. However, if a student consistently uses simple, present-tense verb forms when the past or future is required, or if the various tenses are used randomly, comprehensibility can deteriorate. Since a preponderance of simple verb forms in a non-native speaker's speech may be associated in a listener's mind with her or his intelligence, the speaker's credibility may suffer as well. Calling

ESL students' attention to this aspect of their speech and playing recorded samples of their speeches by way of illustration may be the quickest method to solve the problem.

As with pronouns, correct verb-form usage is an area of English that most ESL students are familiar with from their language courses. Again, however, because the tense and conjugation systems in English are relatively simple compared with those of many other languages, non-native speakers can grow casual about them and may neglect them in speech.

In addition, while the psychological pressure of public speaking is bad enough for native speakers, it can be even worse for all but the most proficient non-native speakers. Syntax may be the first part of the language to fall by the wayside when the ESL student is preoccupied with all the other demands of speechmaking: apprehension, remembering to maintain audience eye contact, and the nonverbal considerations mentioned in Chapter 2, plus the cognitive load of organizing and encoding the message content of the speech itself. It's no wonder that syntactic accuracy often takes a backseat.

IDIOM, SLANG, AND JARGON

International students often find idiomatic expressions and slang the most difficult parts of a new language to learn. This is due not only to the semantic problems involved (e.g., "Let's drop this and move on to the next point" has little to do with the literal meaning of *drop*), but also to the social appropriateness of colloquial language. While most adult native speakers of any language have a finely honed sensitivity to the tolerance level of a given social situation for the use of colloquial language, non-native speakers often do not. They may be unaware of the social cues that signal the appropriate level of formality in a given social situation. As a result, they may avoid using colloquial expressions altogether, giving their English a stilted, overly formal quality, or they may use such expressions at inopportune moments. Colloquial speech is important to speaker ethos, and may also affect the social environment in the classroom. The correct use of colloquialisms may boost a non-native English speaker's credibility when speaking to audiences made up of mostly native English speakers, and may also positively impact the effectiveness of pathos.

You, as the speech instructor, are well advised to let each ESL student establish his or her own comfort level with colloquial English. This is a part of the language that is gradually acquired as learners become acculturated to a new language community; thus, students themselves are the best judges of how formal or informal they wish to appear to their audiences. However, you can serve as a cultural informant, letting students know when they have misused particular idiomatic expressions in their speeches and how they can use them properly. You can also provide students with the idiomatic meta-language of speechmaking — that is, the special expressions that public speakers use to help keep their audience on track (e.g., "Let me start off by saying that . . . ," "Let's turn now to . . . ," "I'd like to close by . . ."). These colloquial organizational markers or "signposts" can be fundamental for effective speech organization for all speakers, and may be particularly helpful for improving the comprehensibility of speeches by non-native English speakers.

Jargon is another feature of language that can challenge native and non-native speakers of English alike. Jargon can have a positive or negative effect; for example, it produces insider status for those who use it correctly, but it can function to exclude those who do not know it. Students need to be reminded that any jargon they use in speeches, whether it is related to a profession, hobby, or other activity, needs to be defined for their audience.

SPEECH RATE

Speech rate is a fluency issue. Along with pronunciation, it is one of the first elements of an ESL speech that attracts the attention of a native-speaking audience. Think of speech rate as a continuum, with a distracting number of pauses and hesitations at one extreme, contrasted with breakneck speed on the other. Somewhere in the middle of the continuum lies the ideal speech rate that audiences find most comprehensible. ESL students should be encouraged to aim for that point. This is important from a speech content point of view as well, since the amount of material they are able to deliver within the set time limits of a speech should not differ greatly from that of their native-speaking classmates.

ESL students with limited experience speaking English may fall near the slower end of the spectrum. They may simply not have had enough language practice to achieve a normative speech rate. Or their vocabulary knowledge may be so deficient that they are engaged in extended mental word searching. Such students may simply not be ready for a speech class geared toward native speakers and might best be referred to an English-language support program. Other students, whose slow speech rate is more a function of personal or culturally preferred style than lack of knowledge of English, can be coached to increase their speed by having them read aloud portions of a text at a faster rate than they are accustomed to. With your help, they can calibrate their speech rate to an appropriate level. At home, they can practice their speech with a recorder, focusing on eliminating distracting pauses and increasing their speed.

At the other end of the speech-rate continuum are students who are sufficiently comfortable with English, but whose nervousness pushes them to race through their material. Excessive rate combined with pronunciation inaccuracies can render their speeches nearly incomprehensible. In these cases, techniques appropriate for use with native speakers can be used with ESL students as well: for example, writing explicit cues on their speech cards to "speak slowly!" and marking specific points in their notes where they should pause to take a deep breath or take a drink of water.

Fast speaking is more normative in some cultures and languages than in others, and also may relate to speaker identity management. Our Venezuelan friend, for example, has an extraordinary knowledge of the English language, writes beautiful and sophisticated academic prose, and is fully bilingual though she has heavily accented English even after living in the United States for decades. She argues that she has reduced her accent as much as she can without slowing her speech so much that she no longer feels herself. That is, speaking quickly is part of her personality and identity that she is not willing to compromise simply to reduce her accent.

You may find that excessive speech rate in ESL speakers may correct itself as the course progresses. On the other hand, as with other linguistic problems mentioned previously, explicit coaching — plus providing the students with recorded evidence from their own speeches — may be necessary in order to make them aware of the issue. In one training technique, too-fast ESL speakers are provided with a model recording in which a native speaker speaks at an ideal rate. In a practice session, the student plays back the recording with one finger on the pause button. After each sentence, the student pauses the recording and "shadows" the phrase, consciously slowing his or her natural rate to match that of the speaker.

In the end, it is not your responsibility to solve all ESL students' English-language problems. However, in order to increase students' chances for success in the public speaking class, and to help them enhance their credibility as speakers, it does fall on you as the instructor to identify your students' most salient linguistic issues, make them aware of specific areas that need work, and then devise a practice strategy that students can use on their own. In extreme cases, it may fall on the instructor to identify early on those students whose English-speaking ability is simply not up to the demands of the course, and to counsel them to delay taking the course until after greater fluency is achieved through other available means. For most ESL students, however, early diagnosis followed by a combination of coaching and independent practice can bring the language issues discussed here under control so that students can turn their attention to other, more content-related issues of successful speechmaking. While this book was designed to support the instructor's management of issues related to non-native English speakers in their public speaking classes, it is also your responsibility and a real opportunity to raise all students' consciousness about the many variations of spoken English they will encounter in their everyday lives, and the importance of their openness and competence as listeners.

CLASSROOM ACTIVITIES

Ask students about all the languages that they speak, that are spoken in their homes, and that they have studied. Ask them to share any experiences they have had making presentations in a non-native language and to discuss the specific challenges of doing so. Take the opportunity to interpret students' examples in relation to the various linguistic concepts in this chapter.

Ask students to consider how they think monolingualism versus multilingualism might affect speaker choices and audience reception. Use this opportunity to discuss issues such as pronunciation, accent, fluency, and speech rate as they affect *both* native and non-native speakers of English, and how they may affect *both* speaker choices and audience reception.

Have students generate a list of homonyms, writing them on the board. Discuss how these words may be confusing for non-native English speakers, and generate strategies for ensuring clarity in speech situations.

Have students work in dyads or small groups to generate examples of slang and colloquial terms and phrases. Have them write down each term or phrase, and discuss the cultural information embedded in it. Then generate a large-group discussion of the examples they found, taking the opportunity to explore how slang and colloquialisms can affect speaker credibility or relatability and audience understanding.

Invite students to share an example of a tongue twister from their childhood. The instructor should offer one or two examples (e.g., "She sells seashells by the seashore"). Encourage international students to share examples from their own languages. Discuss why tongue twisters are funny. Discuss how they can be used to develop speech fluency and strong enunciation in preparation for presentations. Also point out how language choice in a speech can contribute to speaker fluency, regardless of whether one is a native or non-native speaker, because some sentences are easier to say than others.

CHAPTER

4

Planning the Speech

The previous chapters were concerned primarily with the conceptual and linguistic issues that may complicate instruction in the culturally diverse public
speaking classroom. Chapters 4 through 6 relate more to practical concerns and
are designed to help you understand the unique problems and approaches ESL
and other diverse students might take in speech preparation, as well as to help
you guide them in their choices.

To avoid ethnocentrism in this endeavor — to resist the temptation to "fix"
ESL and linguistic minority students or to teach them the "correct" way — we
encourage an approach that relies on audience analysis. While ESL and other
diverse students may have legitimate differences in rhetorical purpose, content,
and style, their native rhetorical strategies may or may not be appropriate or
effective with all U.S. audiences. Because in many colleges and universities the
majority of the classroom will be U.S. students whose first language is English,
all students are typically expected to address their speeches to this audience.
On the other hand, with growing diversity in many colleges and universities,
particularly public schools in states like Arizona, California, New Mexico, and
Texas, some courses may not have a distinguishable majority group.

To the extent that your class has a different composition, you can adjust
this approach accordingly. For instance, in teaching public speaking in Spain to
a class comprised of Spanish, other international, and American study-abroad
students, one of the authors developed assignments asking students to use and
explain the rhetorical conventions of students' home and host cultures. The
goal in engaging linguistically diverse students is to highlight intentionality
in relation to student choices based largely on their rhetorical aims and their
audiences.

A CROSS-CULTURAL VIEW OF RHETORIC

A senator announces his candidacy for the presidency. A corporate CEO gives
a PowerPoint presentation to her organization's board of directors. A farmer
stands up at his local co-op meeting to protest the latest changes in govern-
ment subsidy practices. For Americans, these might all seem to be "normal"
public speaking situations. However, for students from a variety of other
countries, political systems, geographical locales, religious backgrounds, and
cultural practices, scenarios like these might seem less common, while others
may be more typical and familiar. Instructors in diverse classrooms should

remember that cultures vary significantly in regard to who speaks publicly, under what circumstances, using which stylistic norms, and with what ideal outcomes.

Consider these alternative scenarios. In Warm Springs Indian culture, it is typical for tribal members to gather in community meetings, but individuals may not be allowed to speak for themselves in these meetings—especially not women or young people. Under these circumstances, it is appropriate to ask someone older (usually male) to speak on one's behalf. Further, nonverbal communication (accompanying facial and body movement as well as paralinguistic variation) may be virtually imperceptible to the outside observer. Similarly, in some Asian cultures and under some circumstances, mediators are used to make presentations in formal speaking arenas. Nonverbal behaviors in more collectivistic, high-context cultures may or may not accurately reveal the speaker's emotional state. One of our students from Botswana, for example, who was studying agriculture and was required to take the public speaking course, anticipated returning home to instruct his village in new agricultural techniques, where few had formal education. During one of the authors' trips to El Salvador, a local mayor gave a speech to visiting Americans about the peace process in his region of the country, then emerging from a protracted civil war. He was later detained by national officials and relieved of his political post. These examples remind us that international students come from incredibly diverse public speaking contexts, where the rules for speaking publicly and the consequences for doing so can vary significantly. A process of adaptation is central to effective public speaking.

One way of teaching public speaking is to use Lloyd Bitzer's model of "the rhetorical situation." In this model, the underlying assumption is that speaking arises from situations. In other words, the prevailing problems and needs of a community actually *create* the opportunity and necessity for public discourse. This model has decidedly Western roots and for some international students may seem unusual or difficult to adapt to their own contexts. While many U.S. students may take for granted the importance of public speaking in political and professional life, opportunities for public speaking can vary tremendously across cultures.

The varied experience of some students, the relative inexperience of others, and the apathetic attitude of some U.S. students all create a similar opportunity for instructors. Many of us take a civic education approach to teaching public speaking, treating participation in discourse on issues of public importance as a right and a responsibility in a participatory democracy. In today's public speaking classroom, such an approach should be explained rather than taken for granted. While such an approach might be new to some international students, it offers them an opportunity to discuss and share the opportunities and the constraints on public discourse in their home countries. Similarly, many U.S. minority students may find the civic education approach idealistic and disingenuous, depending upon their sense of enfranchisement and experience with U.S. institutions.

SETTING UP THE RHETORICAL SITUATION

As an instructor, you should not assume that all students understand the fundamental nature of the public speaking assignment. In addition to individual assignment criteria, you may want to talk about the varied reasons for, and the benefits of, public speaking. Most texts introduce the topic of public speaking with a discussion of academic and career expectations, general communication skills, specific presentational skills, civic duty, and leadership potential, all of which can be enhanced by a public speaking course. In this way, students may identify their own needs, perhaps reconciling their own cultural norms with chosen academic paths, career expectations, and so on. This might be done through a combination of class discussion and self-reflection.

In order to create a meaningful speaking opportunity, you might ask students to assess the rhetorical situation presented by the classroom itself (as opposed to that of the larger social context). This is part of any audience-analysis exercise, but focuses specifically on the composition of each class. What are the problems faced in this "community"? What constraints exist that might impede message effectiveness? What are the interests of this audience, and what types of action can members of this audience take? Many U.S. students may think they understand the classroom setting and audience but may not have examined their tacit assumptions about it, while international students might have variant understandings; both can benefit from this explicit process of audience analysis. In this way, international students can get to know their American audience better, and U.S. students can become more aware of (and hopefully sensitive toward) their culturally and linguistically diverse classmates.

CHOOSING A TOPIC

The audience-analysis exercise is very likely to reveal that the diverse students know little about each other's countries and customs. This is a wonderful opportunity to create an informative speech assignment around these topics. International students may feel more comfortable beginning their foray into public speaking with a speech about their home country, for example. As the instructor, you might encourage this for a number of reasons.

First, these speeches can enhance the cultural knowledge of all the students in the class. In a time of immense technological, economic, sociopolitical, and demographic change globally, this is an opportunity to enhance students' awareness. For instance, one of our Israeli students gave a speech on the kibbutz system to help her classmates better understand her experience growing up in Israel.

Second, speeches about home cultural topics allow ESL students to incorporate familiar linguistic and cultural information; the intimidation of the first speech can be reduced if the content is familiar. For example, one of our Mexican-American students spoke about "Spanglish." Given the prevalence of this linguistic phenomenon in the United States, particularly the border area where this particular course was taught, all the students related to his speech, gained appreciation for his accent, and learned about language.

Third, international students often undergo substantial culture shock and acculturation difficulties. The first speech can be an opportunity to revisit the home culture, to bring that experience to the host culture, and perhaps to reconcile some of the discomfort of the cross-cultural transition. One Saudi Arabian student, for example, gave a speech on portrayals of Arabs in Hollywood cinema — portrayals that emphasize wealth, polygamy, and terrorism. In addition to raising the class's consciousness about ethnic/national stereotypes in film, his speech allowed him to process the relationship between mass-media portrayals and the constraints on his own intercultural communication experience. In other words, he felt that U.S. media portrayals of Arabs had created a prejudice in his American classmates that was applied to him personally, and the informative speech gave him the chance to bring this to their attention in a nonconfrontational way.

Some caveats should accompany the preceding recommendations. Just as all students seem to have difficulty in narrowing their topics, international students may feel compelled to take on their entire culture's history in seven to nine minutes. While home-culture topics are worthwhile and appropriate to the audience, they must be limited in scope. It is here that instructors might work particularly diligently with ESL students, who are confronted with the complicating factors of speech fluency, accent, and time constraints. The Israeli student mentioned previously, whose English-language skills were excellent, nevertheless had trouble keeping a speech about the history of U.S.–Israeli relations under twelve minutes. International students may feel compelled to tackle such topics in their speeches because U.S. students know very little about their cultures' histories and customs. Developing exercises in outlining and topic narrowing for these students can thus be very helpful (see Chapter 5).

Another caveat concerns audience analysis. Helping international students through the audience-analysis process may entail more than counseling in topic choice; there are potential intercultural and interpersonal ramifications for the student. An international student may find that alienating the speech audience may result in social alienation, which is contrary to his or her acculturation goals, not just speech goals. For example, one student from a Middle Eastern country wanted to give a speech on why it was better for a man to have several wives. The instructor reminded him that the audience, mostly American women, might not be particularly well disposed toward this topic. Further, in the United States, since polygamy is illegal and contradicts core cultural and moral values, a persuasive speech on this topic would be seen as inappropriate in Bitzer's sense. Nevertheless, the student persisted and was subsequently ostracized by the other students in the class, who reported in peer evaluations that the speaker was chauvinistic and a bit ridiculous in choosing this topic.

Finally, it is important to remember that students should not be expected to speak for or about their culture or identity in ways that assume they have expertise only about these areas but not about more general topics. While choosing a topic related to one's own culture or identity might be a useful initial speaking strategy (i.e., to reduce nervousness or help manage one's cross-cultural transition as discussed earlier), international students should be encouraged to identify topics of general interest, of particular disciplinary relevance, or requiring research and development of logos and ethos unrelated to their cultural or linguistic identity. One goal is to ensure that students' speeches are not used to reinforce cultural stereotypes (e.g., that all Brazilians are experts on soccer). It is equally imperative that majority U.S. students come to see non-native English speakers and those from many racial, ethnic, and national backgrounds as having expertise and authority.

RESEARCHING THE SPEECH

When we talk about speech preparation, we mean doing research and gathering source materials. A class dedicated to library research (discussed in Chapter 2) brings everyone up to speed on the latest search technologies and familiarizes them with the reference desk, materials, and personnel. International students should be reminded that library personnel are available to answer even the most basic questions. Most reference librarians are familiar with basic speech assignments, since the introductory-speech course is a general-education requirement on most campuses. In some cases, the reference librarians may know more about the assignments than the students do. Most library staff are remarkably supportive educators who enjoy helping students explore ideas for and then research their speech topics.

Many of the topics concerned with researching speeches are covered nicely in public speaking textbooks. Identifying different types of sources, the nature of content in these different sources, locating sources, and critically evaluating source content are among the typical areas covered. However, integrating this source material into the speech is an area where ESL students might have particular trouble. In Brazil, for example, students are familiar with the procedures of library research. The reference list of Brazilian students' papers will contain the citations for the works they consulted; however, in our experience there may be no references to these works in the text itself. International and non-native English-speaking students may need explicit instruction in how to integrate source material into the speech according to typical expectations of the U.S.-based classroom. This should include the use of in-speech citation and the related choices for and challenges with doing so. For example, in-speech citation may entail the pronunciation of difficult author names. Instead, students can be instructed in alternative strategies such as citing the journal title or the scientific organization instead of an author who would likely be unfamiliar to the audience anyway. Then the complete citation information can be included in their speech bibliography or on a visual aid. Making wise decisions about when to use direct quotes, how to effectively paraphrase material (and how to cite), and how these practices relate to academic integrity and speaker credibility can be featured in this exploration.

CROSS-CULTURAL RHETORICAL CONVENTIONS

Just as the circumstances of public speaking vary from culture to culture, so too do rhetorical conventions such as organizational patterns, language choice, persuasive strategies, and delivery styles. The first three of these will be discussed here; the latter will be discussed in the next two chapters.

Many of the issues raised in Chapter 2 in relation to learning style are also relevant to speech organization. We discussed how cognitive problem-solving patterns might vary significantly from culture to culture. It is not surprising then that this cognitive variance can manifest itself in speech organization. What we consider a logical development of ideas may not be perceived as logical to all students. Most introductory public speaking texts include explicit instruction in topical, chronological, spatial, causal, and problem-solution organizational approaches. Although this instruction might already be clear for most ESL students, you may want to make an explicit connection between the speech-organization chapter of the text and their logical development of ideas and speech organization. Working with ESL students and their outlines with this chapter of the text may also help students make this connection: that they are being asked to use a *different* form of logic that will be appropriate to *this* audience or to this type of speech act. As mentioned throughout this book, discussion of logical organization should be culturally contextualized for students, not presented as the only correct way to organize thoughts and ideas.

In terms of language choice in speech preparation, as the instructor, you may again confront the issue of directness versus indirectness. For members of some cultures, direct and concrete language might be seen as confrontational rather than clear. Being too concrete with one's utterances may be seen as disrupting group harmony and a challenge to "face" by some students from Eastern cultures. Some African American students may orient around an oral tradition that is characterized by the effective use of innuendos, inferences, and circumlocution to make a point. In the Anglo-American tradition of forthrightness, though not all U.S.–born students value this approach in the same way, these alternative strategies might be considered ineffective or unclear. Exercises in the use and value of concrete language early in the semester can help all public speaking students and may particularly be helpful for ESL students in the development of their vocabulary.

By contrast, the use of vivid language may be more of a challenge for some U.S. students in a contemporary university climate characterized by apathy. These students may need assistance choosing language that reflects more passion for and engagement with their speech topics. International students may come from cultures where poetry and storytelling are central to the rhetorical tradition. Of course, this is another area where ESL students may encounter difficulty with the time constraints of the public speaking assignment. In any event, emphasis on precise word choice as well as on the effective use of vivid language is likely to help all speakers.

Just as what is considered "logical" may vary from culture to culture, so may the norms and expectations for effective persuasion. Generally, Westerners learn that all claims must be supported with some type of evidence, and that some claims are best supported with statistical or scientific evidence. While we have trouble holding our public officials to this standard, we remain committed to teaching our introductory public speaking students the importance of supportive evidence. Some international students may not initially feel compelled to use or cite evidence in their speech. They might find it more persuasive to use alternative strategies. Saudi Arabians, for example, have a preference for eloquence and historical reference, which they may consider more persuasive than cold facts. One African American rhetorical tradition emphasizes boasting as a means of building credibility and may not be deemed effective by all audience members. We have found that many of our Chinese and Japanese students, by stark contrast, tend to avoid mention of their own accomplishments, thus making it difficult for them to establish their expertise in a speech. As with all of the cultural communication research informing this book, we caution against overgeneralization. For example, some culturally preferred rhetorical strategies are employed only within monocultural groups, whereby nonnative speakers or "cultural outsiders" in any particular context may begin to code switch, or adopt more general communication practices rather than culturally specific ones.

Sensitivity to these variations can assist you in addressing the issues of persuasion and credibility in a way that recognizes the cultural variety of attitudes and approaches. For instance, U.S. students can learn much about passion in public speaking from their international counterparts. Arab students might learn the crucial role of factual data for American audiences, and Japanese students might be guided in a variety of ways to build speaker credibility. Discussion of these and other variations in cultural practices and preferences can lead to a productive conversation about ethos, pathos, and logos that is sensitive to cultural differences. It also can point to the rich array of rhetorical choices to consider depending on the rhetorical situation.

While discussion of cultural differences is an important part of embracing and leveraging the learning opportunities of a diverse classroom environment, it is important to do so without reinforcing stereotypes of individual students. Managing the tension between generalization and individualization comprises one of the central instructional challenges in teaching intercultural communication, and this holds similarly true for teaching in multicultural contexts.

CLASSROOM ACTIVITIES

Explore the notion of exigency by having students identify recent public speeches or presentations that they have witnessed, trying to generate examples from a variety of cultural contexts. Ask students to identify the importance of the speaker's topic to the particular audience and the purpose of the speech in relation to that audience.

Using Bitzer's model, ask the students to brainstorm topics that would be appropriate to the rhetorical situation of your classroom. What relevant issues or topics in students' public and personal lives might also matter to others in the class? Given the diversity in this classroom, what topics would students like to learn about from one another?

After brainstorming possible topics, have students explore which topics generated are appropriate for upcoming assignments (that is, well-suited for informative versus demonstrative versus persuasive speaking) and which relate well to their own credibility, passion, expertise, and access to research (and its conferred expertise).

Choose one topic from the brainstorming exercise and have students work in groups. Each is assigned a different audience (assign a diversity of audiences and settings) and must identify specific adaptations a speaker would employ to ensure that the topic is relevant to each audience.

Return to the examples of recent speeches generated by the students and explore speaker credibility. Use the following kinds of questions to guide exploration: Why did you find the speaker credible (or not)? What did you notice about the speaker's vocabulary that contributed to (or detracted from) speaker credibility? How did the speaker establish his/her expertise, accomplishments, and credentials? How will you establish your credibility to an audience with whom you lack familiarity?

Pick a topic of shared concern to students, such as the costs of parking on campus, or availability of public transportation around campus. Have students evaluate the rhetorical situation: Who is the audience? Where do they stand: indifferent, supportive of your perspective? What do they already know about the topic? What questions do you need answered in the speech? What is the goal of the speech?

Arrange to spend one class session in the library. Have students work in pairs or groups on a "scavenger hunt" for sources around a particular speech topic (assigned by instructor). Give students a time limit to return with one to three different types of sources on the topic. Engage in an analysis of the quality of those sources, their different characteristics in relation to constructing effective arguments or evidence about the topic, and how to cite each source in a speech.

5

Practicing the Speech

During a summer when one of the authors taught in China, he walked to class each morning through a small garden in Beijing frequented by men practicing tai chi. There were also twenty or thirty young people, each one standing alone and facing one of the many trees, reading aloud. They all stood at different angles to the trees; there was no recognizable pattern. Most looked down into their books, their faces only four inches or so from the pages and their heads just four inches or so from the trunks of the trees. During the first week of the semester, the author pondered to himself why these young people were awake at such an early hour, talking so privately to the trees.

One day he recognized one of his students, following the same path he was walking on, holding in her hands a small book. He tentatively asked her what these young people were doing as he gestured discreetly toward the others reading to trees. She looked at him at first as if he were asking her to reveal a secret. He backed away from her slowly and whispered, "Is it something religious?" She looked at him for a moment with a serious expression and then began to giggle. "No," she said. "They are practicing their English."

As he and his student walked through the garden together, toward the general direction of the building that housed their classroom, she explained to him that not only was the fresh air good for the young people's working minds, but, more important, the trees didn't laugh when they made mistakes. In the Chinese garden, they could talk as loudly as they wished, conversing with the trees without the fear they often experienced in the traditional classroom.

Even more than native English-speaking students, ESL and other linguistically diverse students benefit from sustained and systematic oral practice. Speech practice not only helps allay the students' natural apprehensions about speaking in public, as the Chinese students found in the narrative above, but it also can help resolve some of the language issues discussed in previous chapters. In this chapter, we suggest a set of practice techniques that we have found to be effective in helping linguistically diverse students improve the quality of their speeches.

COMPENSATORY STRATEGIES

The practice strategies we recommend here are based on the notion of compensation; it is unreasonable to expect a typical ESL student to make dramatic gains in English-language proficiency over one semester in a public speaking class or even as a result of individual tutoring. Therefore, the most efficient route is for students to develop a set of compensatory, discourse-based strategies that will make their presentations clear and easy to follow, despite lapses (even substantial problems) in pronunciation, grammar, and vocabulary. This can be accomplished by guiding students through four practice phases: (1) developing linguistic self-awareness; (2) directed feedback; (3) preparation of speaking notes; and (4) fluency practice. We explore how various uses of technology can provide an additional compensatory strategy in Chapter 7.

Linguistic Self-Awareness

Some ESL students may be excessively critical of their own speaking ability, unnecessarily raising their level of apprehension. Others may overestimate their own effectiveness simply by virtue of having survived, and even excelled in, previous English-language situations. Thus, it is crucial for ESL students to have a realistic picture of their actual performance ability as soon after the first assigned speech as possible. Although they may have formed a general, overall impression of their classmates' abilities from listening to the first round of speeches, they may find it more difficult to view their own performances objectively without directed, individualized feedback.

The best way for ESL speakers, as well as speakers of global English varieties that are heavily accented from the perspective of U.S. English speakers, to develop an accurate linguistic self-image is through a combination of reviewing recorded performances and receiving directed feedback. If possible, the students' initial speeches should be video recorded. Native English-speaking students may receive adequate feedback through oral and written evaluations from the instructor and their peers, but linguistically diverse students will find it more difficult to highlight problem areas and make significant improvements in their speeches without direct, firsthand evidence of their strengths and weaknesses. That said, all students benefit by viewing their recorded speeches, and instructors should make clear in their syllabi and instructions whether recording speeches is required or merely recommended. The same rules should hold true for all students in the course, in order not to problematize the speech learning of NNSSAE and international students.

Ideally, these students should first have an opportunity to view their recorded speeches alone. Many will never have seen themselves speaking before, let alone in English, and a solo viewing opportunity will help them get past the initial shock, and perhaps some embarrassment, of seeing themselves in action. When assigned to preview the recording, students should be asked to make an informal assessment of their own performance. A simple way for them to accomplish this is to write down three positive assessments about their speech and three aspects that they would like to improve in preparation for the next presentation. Their responses form the agenda for the next step in the practice sequence: an initial student/instructor conference. While many students will highlight linguistic elements such as those discussed in Chapter 3, you might encourage them to identify at least one more general strength and challenge (that is, those unrelated specifically to language issues). This can ensure that linguistically diverse students are attending to their rhetorical choices and seeing the development of effective speaking as something much broader than language fluency alone.

Directed Feedback

Most instructors use a speech-evaluation rubric to give feedback and assign grades to their students. We suggest supplementing this with a simple, four-category sheet specifically designed for non-native English-speaking students. The four categories are *accent, rate, grammar,* and *organizational markers* (as discussed in Chapter 3, these are idiomatic phrases and sentences that often function as signposts for the audience). You may wish to alter or add to these categories as you work with your students, based on specific issues or observations you have made. The supplemental sheet can be completed during the ESL students' speeches or later while viewing the recording with the student during the conference. These rubrics should be made available to students for use in their planning and practice.

Once ESL students have previewed their own recorded speeches, they should schedule an initial conference in order to view the recording with you as the instructor and discuss specifically the items on the supplemental form. The conference should begin with a discussion of the student's own self-evaluation; this gives the student the freedom to set the agenda for the conference and to begin taking responsibility for his or her progress in the course. Hearing the student's responses also helps you gauge the level of the student's linguistic self-awareness. Students who are too hard on themselves will benefit from some reassurance and positive reinforcement. On the other hand, students with a complacent view of their own performance need direct, frank, but still supportive feedback from you to bring their expectations in line with your goals for the next speech. Again, as with recordings of speeches, conferences should be made available to all students. Many instructors require a conference with each student following their first speech, and this advice follows from our recommendations about office hours in Chapter 1.

The second part of the conference consists of giving the student detailed feedback based on the four categories from the supplemental sheet. Before playing the recording, discuss the four categories in turn; in each category, provide both general feedback and specific suggestions for areas where you wish the student to focus attention. Then, with the recording being viewed, cover these problem areas again, this time in the context of the ongoing speech. The recording may be paused and replayed at critical points along the way. This two-stage feedback process is important; much oral language behavior takes place below the level of full awareness, so students benefit from developing conscious knowledge of the problem areas before they are expected to recognize them in the context of the speech.

It is important to prioritize the comments and corrections selected for discussion, as ESL students can be overwhelmed by an overly thorough analysis of their oral language problems. Choose those areas that are most in need of improvement, and save finer points for later work. A general focus on audience comprehensibility and speech effects can help keep students oriented towards their speaking goals as motivation for linguistic improvement. After all, this is a public speaking course, not an English language course.

Under the category of *accent* should be included only those aspects of pronunciation, stress, and intonation that seriously interfere with the student's intelligibility. You may not feel comfortable at first making generalizations for students about their articulation and voicing of sounds; however, individual words and phrases that are obscured due to mispronunciation can be identified. Key words that are habitually mispronounced in the speech are prime targets for correction, and a list of problem words can be developed during the conference for students to practice on their own. Incidental pronunciation errors are better left untreated. It is worth emphasizing to students during individual conferences that communication effectiveness does not require perfect English. While accented speech requires more attentive listening, it may be useful to point out, as well, that a student's accent can create heightened interest for the listener, and may contribute to the memorability of the speech.

The second category, *rate*, is a feature of speech that ESL students are unlikely to be aware of as they are speaking. Thus, it is important that you as the instructor call attention to a rate that is either so fast that it makes comprehension difficult for the audience, or so slow as to be distracting to the audience. You should point students to practice techniques outlined in Chapter 3. Inviting students to practice very slow delivery or very fast delivery prior to settling at the "just right" pacing can bring greater awareness to the issue of speech rate. It also may be worth reminding ESL students that all students struggle with pacing due to nervousness, as well as having the wrong amount of content for the speech time frame.

In filling out the *grammar* portion of the supplemental form, remember that the great majority of grammatical errors made by non-native speakers of English in their oral performance will pass by native speakers unnoticed. It is best to focus the student's attention only on those syntactic mistakes that seriously distort or confuse the meanings they are trying to convey, such as word-order reversals or the omission of major sentence elements. Other noticeable errors mentioned in Chapter 3 include confusions of gender and number in pronouns (*he* instead of *she*, or either of these instead of *they*) or dropping pronouns altogether. Simple present tense verbs substituted for the past tense also should be corrected given the likelihood that these mistakes can lead to confusion among listeners. Keep in mind that alerting students to too many syntactical-error categories increases the cognitive load they are already struggling under and may actually increase their problems with fluency and speech apprehension.

Organizational markers, as discussed in Chapter 3, are those phrases that speakers use to signal to their audience where they are in their speech and where they intend to go next (e.g., "Next let me turn to . . . ," "Now that we've seen how . . . ," "Let's go on to look at . . ."). Fluent, practiced speakers often dispense with these oral signposts, since they can have a (sometimes false) sense of confidence that their audience will be carried along by the inherent logic of their topic development and their overall coherence. Sometimes paralinguistic cues such as altered pacing, voice tone, and sentence cadence also can function effectively as signposts for native English speakers and those with accents most familiar to the audience. Non-native English speakers, on the other hand, likely will find that the use of formal markers can help compensate for language problems that may obscure important transition points in their speeches. During the individual conference, you can pause the recording at these critical junctures and suggest suitable organizational markers to be inserted. Students should also be instructed to listen for examples of such phrases in the speeches of their native English-speaking classmates. As with troublesome pronunciation items, these phrases should be noted and filed away by the student for use in later speeches. It may be worth highlighting for non-native speakers that all speakers can benefit from developing repertoires of speech choices such as organizational markers.

Preparation of Speaking Notes

A clear organizational outline is essential for ESL students if they are to maximize their speech performance. It is also an invaluable aid for practice prior to a class presentation. As we know from our work with native English-speaking students, confusing, hard-to-follow presentations may be as much a result of inadequate speaking notes as of English-language problems. In some cases, a poor speech may be the result of both. Training in outlining and notecard preparation may already be included as part of your work with students; but even if it is, you should not assume that ESL students in your class are familiar with these techniques or that they can use them effectively. In fact, for many non-native speakers, the public speaking class may be their first experience with formal outlining.

The first speech assignment, often relatively informal (e.g., an introductory speech during the first or second week of class), offers the opportunity to assess students' organizational habits. Some students may have no notes at all and may have attempted to deliver the first speech from memory, a common oral strategy in many parts of the world. Alternatively, you may find that some ESL students may have written out their entire first speech word for word in the form of a transcript. This is a technique that is guaranteed to exaggerate existing problems with pronunciation and with word and sentence stress. Neither of these techniques is likely to result in a speech delivered in the optimal style desired in most public speaking courses in the United States: a fluent, extemporaneous delivery that has the appearance of "fresh talk," but that is in fact carefully planned and rehearsed.

Whether the student uses a single-sheet outline or converts the outline into a set of notecards is unimportant; what is important is that the notes contain a clear thesis statement and an ordered set of topics, subtopics, and supporting material. Once ESL students have been guided through this procedure, they should begin to realize the value of their notes not only as a rehearsal aid, but also as an essential support for in-class presentations. It is a good idea, therefore, to ask to see ESL students' notes for the speech in advance of delivery to determine whether this is an area where they need support. Some instructors require all students to provide an outline in advance of the speaking day, or just prior to the speech — a strategy that is likely to hold all students accountable for the written quality of their speech preparation and to enhance your ability to assess whether speech delivery issues are organizational (rather than linguistic).

As mentioned in Chapter 4, students' challenges with effective outlining may be rooted in cultural differences as to what constitutes the logical development of ideas. Outlining preparation can help ESL students create speeches that better match their American audience's expectations for organization. It is important to stress audience orientation to a critique of ESL students' speech organization, rather than merely characterizing their speeches as poorly organized.

Practice for Fluency

The downside of individual conferencing is that it is time-consuming and highly directive. You will probably be able to meet with each ESL student only a limited number of times during the course, but even at that rate, students can all too easily become dependent on you as a helpful instructor. The best way to avoid an overcommitment of time, overly dependent students, or both, is to help them establish an at-home practice regimen that will shift the responsibility to them for achieving their own success in the public speaking class. The most effective practice regimen is one that involves overpractice and multiple audiences.

The benefit of overpractice for ESL students cannot be exaggerated. While overpreparation can make presentations by native English speakers seem stiff and memorized, ESL students should be encouraged to practice a new speech several times in front of different audiences: alone, with a friend or two for feedback, and at least once with a tape recorder. Today most students have smartphones, which can be very useful for this purpose. Repeated practice helps students get accustomed to speaking from their notes and allows them to time their speech. If they run over or under the allotted time, they can use subsequent practices to squeeze or stretch the speech as necessary. Repeated rehearsals also help students get comfortable using any visual aids that they incorporate into the presentation. Most important, repeated practice increases fluency and self-confidence and reduces the nervousness that inevitably builds up prior to the speech date.

During practice sessions, students should be strongly encouraged to refer to the supplemental feedback sheet you have prepared, as well as to any available peer evaluations. This will help them avoid the same pronunciation errors, delivery problems, and so on in the next speech. Negative feedback should be given when students fail to incorporate repeated suggestions into their subsequent speeches. In this way, they learn that your feedback is valuable and that steady progress is the expected outcome of the extra attention and effort extended to the student during individual conferencing.

The ultimate goal of assisting ESL students to establish an at-home practice regimen is to make them as self-sufficient as any other student in the class. Although they may require extra individual conferencing early in the course, they should eventually be performing as well as their classmates with no extra assistance.

STYLE AND ATTITUDE

Public speaking styles differ from culture to culture, and ESL students, especially international students, sometimes bring with them a manner of delivery that may be appropriate and even highly effective in their own countries but that falls flat with American audiences. Often, this results from the student's having imported into the speech class a very formal style used more commonly in public speaking situations back home, but that may seem stilted, distant, and artificial by American standards. On the other hand, some undergraduate non-native English speakers may over-read the relative casualness of the American classroom and may deliver their first speech in an offhand or overly improvised manner.

In either case, part of the individual conference time can be used to clarify for the student the stylistic objectives of extemporaneous speech and the necessity for careful preparation and practice. In early assignments, the goal is to be conversational in tone yet highly prepared, making genuine connections with the audience and meeting the expectations of the genre in the culture in which the speech is delivered. Exemplars drawn from the other students in the class can be pointed to as models of good public speaking according to American style. Speech delivery will be discussed at greater length in Chapter 6.

It is also instructive to record any question-and-answer session following the speech to see how the ESL students perform in what may be yet another unfamiliar situation. Ad-lib discussions can be more difficult for native speakers of other languages to negotiate than the prepared speech itself, due to listening comprehension difficulties, the need to respond rapidly to questions, and the unexpected nature of the questions asked. Some international students may be put off by being asked pointed questions, and they may respond initially with a hostile or defensive attitude. If this is the case, the student needs to be made aware that questioning is an accepted and expected part of public speaking in the United States. It must be accommodated with good grace and can be prepared for by anticipating the kinds of questions that are likely to be asked. Non-native English speakers who can successfully negotiate the question-and-answer part of their public speaking assignments may make an especially favorable impression on their audience.

CLASSROOM ACTIVITIES

Create an ungraded first speech assignment designed to allow students to view the room from the podium and work on foundational skills such as eye contact, introduction, pace of delivery, facial expressions and gestures, and conclusion. These might have four to five sentences of content (e.g., about how/why they chose their academic major, what they did over the summer, or plans for their first internship). This is a low-stakes opportunity for the instructor to provide initial assessment of all students, and to identify students who may need out-of-class work on linguistic issues.

Discuss the use of outlines and notecards during speech delivery. Share examples of sparse and elaborated notecards; discuss what should and should not be included in these notes (e.g., transliteration of hard-to-pronounce words). Have students prepare a single notecard for their ungraded speech assignment.

Invite the class to generate a list of organizational markers or speech signposts. Write the many examples on the screen (or board) and ask students to organize them into categories (e.g., those that introduce ideas, serve as transitions, signal conclusions, and so on). Discuss the value of signposts and the risks of leaving them out. Explore challenges associated with making them too obvious and explicit or with their overuse. Discuss how they help put the audience at ease and enhance speech memorability. This exercise will enhance ESL speakers' repertoire of linguistic choices and all speakers' organizational choices.

Pair students in an activity designed to help them learn to cite their sources in oral presentations. Have each student bring in at least one source for an upcoming speech assignment and prepare a very short portion of his or her speech in which this source is referenced. Students should take turns presenting an idea based on that source using different methods of in-speech citation (direct quote, paraphrase, summary) and using different bibliographical aspects of the citation (e.g., date, author[s], publication, sponsoring organization, etc.). Discuss effective choices and varied approaches to citation, along with how these practices manifest academic integrity and enhance speaker credibility. This is an opportunity to discuss the challenges of pronouncing difficult jargon terms or author names and speech choices that may provide acceptable alternatives.

Invite students to practice their rate of speaking by using a timed reading of a selected paragraph provided by the instructor. The selected passage might focus on an intercultural topic and/or include difficult-to-pronounce words and names for both native and non-native English speakers. Each student should try reading the paragraph aloud while another student keeps time. Students can discuss different paces and their relative effectiveness for comprehensibility, related to issues such as accent, articulation, and enunciation.

When inviting students for one-on-one conferences, ask them to prepare in advance to ensure it is a productive meeting. Students should view their recorded speech in advance and prepare a written list of strengths and challenges. ESL students might be well served to watch their speech with a peer to help them generate a list that focuses on audience-centered issues (rather than self-perceived insecurities).

6

Delivering the Speech

This chapter covers the key elements of public speaking delivery emphasized in most courses: extemporaneous style, vocal effectiveness, nonverbal communication, and the use of visual aids. We also discuss expectations for audience verbal and nonverbal behavior during speeches. While these recommendations are tailored to the needs of international students and linguistic minority students in the United States, most are also relevant to all beginning public speaking students.

PUBLIC SPEAKING STYLE

Depending on their major area of study as well as their background, most students will be cognizant of three common speech-delivery styles: manuscript, memorization, and extemporaneous. While U.S. students will be familiar with impromptu speaking, international students may find this style unfamiliar and even uncomfortable. It may be worthwhile to introduce impromptu speaking in ungraded speech assignments early in the semester because this is an important organizational and business communication skill that should be acquired by all public speaking students. Part of impromptu speaking is getting over the stage fright of being put on the spot, and part of it is learning to think on one's feet and quickly produce clear and effective remarks. This skill can be particularly challenging for ESL and other linguistic minority students, who rely heavily on advance preparation and practice to overcome potential language barriers based on issues discussed in Chapter 3. While our main goal in beginning public speaking courses is to cultivate effective extemporaneous speaking about substantive issues, we should not underestimate the interpersonal and professional value of impromptu speaking about both trivial and substantive topics. This skill can be particularly valuable for ESL students in demonstrating competency across many contexts.

In most public speaking courses, we spend limited time talking about style with our U.S. students, who are familiar with the cultural norms and for whom the textbook discussion will be clear and relatively self-evident. (Whether or not they can effectively enact these norms and instructions is another matter.) However, the issue of style may be anything but self-evident for many international students. In fact, when we say that effective delivery is "natural," which is often the first feature of extemporaneous speaking highlighted in textbooks, we should remember that very little about the public speaking course content may be experienced as natural for our international and other ESL students.

As with impromptu speaking, extemporaneous speaking may present unique problems for ESL students. Linguistic deficiencies (or low confidence) often cause ESL students to prepare obsessively for assignments, particularly for oral presentations. It is therefore not surprising that ESL students can have a tendency to read their speeches – or to at least want to do so. This directly contradicts the goals of extemporaneous speaking, which is usually the most effective speaking style and the most enjoyable for audiences. It is important to emphasize, once again, that ESL students, whether from international or domestic backgrounds, are not all the same in relation to their attitudes or approaches to delivery.

An example from a beginning Portuguese course might help illustrate some of these issues. This course was designed to enable fluent Spanish speakers to learn Portuguese quickly, and it included several oral presentations. Those students who were struggling with their Portuguese fluency wrote out their presentations and read them to the class, while those students who had achieved strong fluency in Portuguese would simply "wing" their presentations, essentially chatting to the class. This parallels some of the challenges faced by ESL students in the public speaking course. Native-language students, and some partially acculturated ESL students (see Chapter 5), sometimes misinterpret *extemporaneous* to mean *off the cuff* or *spontaneous*, focusing on the dynamic delivery aspects of extemporaneity rather than on the content planning aspects. International students, on the other hand, may focus on the planning side of extemporaneity rather than on the delivery side. This may vary, however, depending on the particular language proficiency of the student. The example of the Portuguese class illustrates that second-language students are not all the same; level of proficiency, particular accent, and home cultural practices all influence attitudes and approach to delivery.

Some cultural differences may additionally affect a student's attitude toward and ability to speak extemporaneously. For instance, when a culture emphasizes a low tolerance for ambiguity (as discussed in Chapter 2), the notion of choosing the exact words of a speech *during* the speech may seem strange and frightening. To at least partially compensate for this, the use of index cards and technology support can allow students to rely on some verbatim passages, while encouraging a more dynamic presentation (as discussed in Chapter 5). Further, with sufficient emphasis on the nonverbal aspects of delivery, students can realize that the words they choose are only part of the overall effectiveness of their presentation.

NONVERBAL BEHAVIOR IN PUBLIC SPEAKING

The nonverbal aspects of speech delivery are supposed to establish speaker credibility, clarify verbal messages, facilitate feedback, and create rapport between the audience and the speaker. Most instructors emphasize how verbal and nonverbal communication work in tandem to create effective messages. For international and ESL students, as well as some U.S. students, however, the nonverbal aspects of speech delivery can very well accomplish the opposite of expected outcomes if they are not consistent with broadly understood and culturally normative behaviors. In addition to the anticipated problems ESL students are likely to face with pronunciation and articulation, it's not difficult to see that other paralinguistic features such as volume, pitch, rate, use of pauses, and vocal variety can present further problems with comprehensibility and effectiveness. Some of these problems may be derived from linguistic issues and others from cultural variability.

Paralinguistic Factors in Delivery

In speech delivery, an effective speaker achieves the "right" volume, including some variability in volume in order to emphasize certain points and changes in emotional reactions to content. For ESL students, perhaps somewhat shy in oral presentation if they lack confidence in their fluency, volume can present a challenge. Further, some students may find it difficult to achieve what U.S.-based audiences deem sufficient volume, whether this is related to gender or cultural norms, or due to lack of confidence. Pitch and rate are equally likely to create hurdles for reasons of linguistic fluency as well as cultural variability. The effective use of pauses, really an art, could turn into speech lag for ESL students, who may pause more frequently for careful pronunciation or for word searching than for effect. Instructors might provide special practice exercises and feedback sessions for these students, as discussed in Chapter 5.

In terms of vocal variety, it is important to remember that speaking cadence varies significantly from language to language. Native English speakers among U.S. audiences tend to find certain cadences and accents, such as those of native French speakers, interesting or charming, and this can work in favor of an ESL student. Instructors may want to prioritize their concerns about paralinguistic speech delivery, since these issues are so closely tied with language proficiency and fluency. It is most important to focus on those issues that create the biggest barriers for comprehensibility for each individual student; these will vary across linguistically diverse individuals.

With facial expressions, eye behavior, gestures, and body posture, instructors might expect international and ESL students to achieve greater adherence to textbook guidelines because these do not appear to depend on language proficiency. Nevertheless, it's important to remember that nonverbal accompaniment to verbal communication varies significantly according to culture (as discussed in Chapter 2). It is important to understand that dealing with the substantial cognitive load necessary to speak in a second language can take up much of an ESL student's capacity for conscious attention, leaving little left over for monitoring their own nonverbal behavior. Such self-monitoring requires a high degree of self-awareness, knowledge, and skill for anyone.

Eye Contact

In public speaking, eye contact is usually considered *the single most important* means of creating rapport with the audience. Yet making eye contact may be a momentous obstacle for some international students. Members of Japanese, Ethiopian, and many American Indian cultures, for example, have very rigid traditional cultural expectations regarding eye contact in relation to who they are, whom they are speaking to, and the context of speaking. Looking up, down, or away might be their culturally appropriate way to communicate focus, show respect, or appear credible. Lacking confidence in the language, or feeling over-all discomfort with the public speaking role (as discussed in Chapter 4), may also reduce the ease of eye contact for some ESL students and is not uncommon for any student with a relatively high degree of communication apprehension.

Early in the course, when nonverbal aspects of public speaking effectiveness are discussed, it would be worthwhile to explore eye contact norms in some detail given the importance of eye contact in public speaking in the United States. Students should be invited to identify the norms in their cultures (and families), as well as variations on formal and informal rules that might relate to a variety of interaction contexts (e.g., among elders, in peer groups, in classrooms, etc.). Students can discuss these norms along with the kinds of sanctions that might accompany rule or norm violations. The goal of discussions like this is not to proscribe strict nonverbal norms for the class, though expectations for effectiveness in a variety of contexts, including your own public speaking class-room, should be part of the discussion. Focus can be placed on raising students' consciousness of their own norms and those of others in the class, to explore students' comfort level with adopting norms different from their own in order to be an effective speaker, and creating audience sensitivity to the kinds of differences your students might manifest in their speeches.

Facial Expressions and Body Movement

Concerns about effective and culturally interpretable facial expressions, gestures, and body movements parallel the concerns about eye contact. Again, we tend to teach that what is "natural" is best, and again, our expectations may not be remotely natural for ESL students. While Americans are noted — and rewarded by audiences — for their friendly smiles, members of other cultures may find these expressions inauthentic or lacking in credibility. Further, we teach that our facial expressions and body language support the emotional content of the speech. Yet the open demonstration of emotion may not be appropriate in some cultures, and emotional displays may be read incorrectly across cultures. For example, Curaçaoan baseball player Andruw Jones has the tendency to smile after he strikes out, a sign of embarrassment. Fans in the American South tended to misinterpret his facial expression to mean that he is cavalier and unserious about his profession, and he received some bad press for this behavior during his tenure on the Atlanta Braves. Interestingly, Andruw Jones is now playing in Japan, where audiences may be more likely to interpret this facial expression correctly.

Although cultural differences in expectations about nonverbal behavior are likely to create difficulties for ESL students in speech delivery, instructors can expect some adoption of the appropriate nonverbal style. We suggest this instruction be embedded in a discussion of cultural differences as much as possible, so that all students can become more aware of the cultural and context variability of these expectations. It is wise to remember, as well, that a lifetime of enculturation will not be overcome in one course, and a high degree of acculturation may not match the goals of all international or ESL students. Instead, instructors can emphasize the importance of students' ability to effectively produce and interpret the wide variety of communication behaviors that they are likely to encounter in the increasingly diverse classroom, workplace, and community environments they will encounter.

USE OF VISUAL AIDS

Generally, instruction in the use of visual aids need not vary greatly for international and ESL students. The recommendations in most textbooks about size, clarity, and arrangement during the speech all apply. Many public speaking students like to use audio or video clips during their speeches. Most U.S. students will be familiar with the technology, but these sorts of resources, so often taken for granted by domestic students and teachers, need to be highlighted for international students, who may not be aware of their availability on campus or may not have received instruction in their use. If you record speeches, you should give international students (as well as any other communicatively apprehensive students) an opportunity to practice in the presence of this technology. Today instructors can assume that their students from most parts of the world are technologically savvy, so the objective is to connect students with campus resources and to illustrate how they can be used effectively in speeches (we discuss this further in Chapter 7).

With respect to flip charts, graphs, and other visual aids, ESL students may require some assistance to be sure that any language contained is accurate and appropriately phrased. While some U.S. students may be quite comfortable paraphrasing and summarizing from PowerPoint slides, less secure ESL students may tend to read visuals verbatim as a way of compensating for linguistic issues. Recognizing this tendency allows us to confront the issue explicitly with ESL students and to explain to them the norms around the use of visual aids. Additionally, given a propensity to speak on cultural subjects, ESL students might be more likely to use costumes, food, and cultural artifacts as visual aids. It would be useful to advise students not to pass out food during speeches and to guard the handling of delicate artifacts. As with all visual aids, the objective is to make sure they enhance, rather than detract from, speech effectiveness.

AUDIENCE COMPORTMENT

We usually focus our instruction in the public speaking classroom on the speakers, a conceptual bias particularly prevalent in the West. But it would be beneficial also to present expectations for appropriate audience behavior, both verbal and nonverbal. Just as speakers should make eye contact with audience members, supportive audience members should meet that eye contact. The same cultural issues apply here as discussed in Chapter 2. Similarly, while in some cultures a call-and-response style of verbal interplay is appropriate during a formal presentation, many U.S. students could find this sort of verbal engagement unusual and disruptive. Again, these issues are best handled as a discussion of cultural variability and a collective negotiation of classroom norms, rather than as a set of "correct" dictums.

Many instructors use peer review of some sort in their public speaking courses. This technique, often supported by a rubric or set of overarching questions, is one way of enforcing better listener engagement during students' speeches, and also gathers more varied feedback for speakers. With a linguistically and culturally diverse classroom, some training in peer review may be worthwhile. We generally have found student feedback to be rather innocuous for the most part, and it may be that preparing feedback informs the reviewers' learning more than it provides useful feedback to the speaker. A discussion of ways to phrase constructive criticism would be valuable for all students, but particularly for international students, who may be unfamiliar with a peer critique model.

CLASSROOM ACTIVITIES

Design a classroom activity in which students practice impromptu speaking. The instructor prepares several topics, and each student picks one from a hat. The student reads the topic and has thirty seconds to prepare a one-minute presentation. The goals are for students to overcome fear, think on their feet, and display effective delivery skills (e.g., eye contact, tone, organizational markers).

Discuss with students the benefits of extemporaneous speaking styles from the perspective of the audience. Have students generate examples of speeches that have been extemporaneous, memorized, and manuscript, and share their thoughts on the strengths and weaknesses of each.

Hand gestures and their meanings can vary tremendously across cultures. Have students share examples from their own culture(s) or from their travels. Discuss how these might affect public speaking situations in some way.

Ask students to generate a list of expectations for audience members during presentations. These should cover posture, facial expressions, eye behavior, and others. Engage a dialogue between the speaker's and the audience member's perspectives on these behaviors. Discuss note-taking as a behavior that might support effective listening and also support Q&A.

Create a practice peer review exercise where students watch a recorded speech and complete a rubric or respond to a set of questions. Invite them to remark on some aspect of the introduction, the organization, and the conclusion, as well as the delivery style. Students can share their feedback. Highlight examples of particularly well-phrased and useful feedback, as well as examples of particularly vague or harsh feedback.

7

Technology: An Integrated Approach

How do skilled communicators use technology? We believe they use it as a tool to enhance their already well-designed presentations. While some public speaking courses may include instruction on how students can upload photos from smartphones and incorporate video files into presentation slides, these "how-to" skills are generally not the central focus of what we do as communication educators. Students, including our linguistically diverse students, are not well served by introductory communication courses that overly emphasize instruction in specific technical skills, many of which have a limited shelf life. In addition, this approach may not work because not all instructors of public speaking are themselves experts in technology.

Because our teaching and learning goals are rooted in the rhetorical foundations of our discipline, it is best to begin any classroom discussion on the topic of technology not by asking *how* we can integrate the latest technology in our presentations, but rather *why* we should do so. Then, if we agree that the circumstances warrant the use of technology for a particular task, we should help students build the necessary skills and confidence to meet the expectations of audiences in their personal and professional lives.

Once students have determined that they understand an assignment, have selected an approach to engage the task, collected relevant research, formulated evidence to support their points, and sufficiently analyzed their audience, their next step is to figure out how best to present the speech. One of these decisions will be whether the presentation should be delivered using technology such as presentation software. Even if the answer to the question is in the affirmative, which it often is, we should continue to remind students that expertise in the latest technology is a poor substitute for skilled execution of the foundational public speaking skills. Technology is always changing; it will not in and of itself make students better speakers if their content is not well organized and well researched and if they are not able to establish their credibility and connect in authentic ways with their audience. Thus, it is indeed an important decision whether *or not* to use technology to meet the audience's needs and expectations.

These days, we all agree that technology-enhanced presentations are the norm in business settings across the globe. In some cases, if presenters choose not to use technology, they risk being perceived not only as less effective, but also as less credible, given those business norms. In view of this, many instructors of public speaking now require their students' speeches to include the use of presentation software such as Microsoft PowerPoint or Apple Keynote in at least one assignment. Additionally, they may ask students to record themselves giving a presentation, to help them learn how to present themselves through a mediated source.

Indeed, exploring technology in the public speaking classroom has multiple benefits. Technology can help our students establish expert status in the classroom and in the workplace. It can help them clarify their messages, share evidence to support their main points, and engage audiences and help them remember content. For linguistically diverse students, technology can provide simultaneous translation, and it can even assist with accent reduction. Technology can augment listening comprehension and make content more organized and the information clearer.

In this chapter, we discuss some of the ways students should prepare to use technology to support and enhance their speeches. We explore the opportunities and challenges of using technology, with special focus on the needs of linguistically diverse students. Instead of providing "how-to" training, we encourage public speaking instructors and their students to consider when technology can and should be used, under what circumstances, with which audiences, and for what purposes. In doing so, we remind instructors and their students that, while there are useful technology tools that can facilitate students' speaking goals, technology should never overshadow the speaker or the speech.

UNDERSTANDING TECHNOLOGY ACCESS AND SKILL LEVEL

As part of their preparation to live, work, and succeed in a multicultural world, there is an expectation that our students need to learn how to use technology. For many instructors, then, the question is not *if*, but *how* to teach students to use technology effectively in our communication courses. While it is ultimately our students' responsibility to make informed choices about their use of technology, it is our responsibility to assist them, to connect them to resources to advance their skills, and to help them make wise decisions about the role of technology in fulfilling their speaking assignments.

Your Class and the Digital Divide

The initial step in this process involves getting to know our students and understanding their past experiences with technology, their current skills with it, their fears and reservations, and the contexts in which they use and plan to use it (personal, academic, and professional). By better understanding their individual needs and goals, we are better positioned to guide our students' learning and help them make the right selection and strategic use of technology to enhance audience engagement, comprehension, and retention of content.

At many colleges and universities, instructors might correctly assume that their students already know how to use relevant technologies before they enroll in a public speaking course. At our university, for example, 98 percent of our undergraduate students report owning a laptop or tablet device, and our library lends such technologies to students who do not already own them. Most of our students update their Facebook status on their smartphones, stream television shows and movies on their tablet devices, and possess at least enough technical knowledge to upload photos to Instagram and videos to YouTube. They are obviously proficient in using technology as consumers — part of a group often referred to as "digital natives."

In fact, starting in high school, many of today's students have been introduced to presentation software such as Prezi, and in some cases, come to college already having significant experience delivering classroom-based presentations that are technologically enhanced. As a result, it is not uncommon for college and university instructors to feel that undergraduate students have more advanced technology skills than we ourselves have. That said, even students from well-resourced high schools — where technology-enhanced presentations were common — may have had little formal discussion of rhetorical theory that undergirds effective speaking. They may even have developed some bad habits whereby flashy presentations with slick production values substitute for substantive and well-supported arguments.

While it may be true that many of our students possess impressive technological skills, it is not safe for us to assume that *all* of our students do, especially in public speaking courses with ESL, international, and student populations from low income households or under-resourced public school districts. For several decades, "the digital divide" has been used as a term to describe inequality among groups in regard to their routine access to and knowledge about basic communication technologies. According to the most recent census data collected in 2011, nearly 76 percent of households in the United States have at least one computer that can access the Internet. However, a closer look at the data reveals that in households described as "U.S. Hispanic," only 58 percent have a computer. Researchers have often pointed to geographical considerations when describing the divide, along with obvious socioeconomic issues. That is, computer ownership and Internet access are also connected with household income. In the United States, for households with annual incomes over $150,000, the rate of computer ownership is 96 percent. For those under $25,000, the rate is 56 percent. Access also varies among international regions. Worldwide, the segment of individuals reporting having access to the Internet is 34 percent; it is only 28 percent in Asia and only 16 percent in Africa.

While the divide is decreasing in the United States between those who have access to a computer and those who do not, scholars who study these matters remind us of related concerns. For example, the second-level digital divide describes the gap between consumers of technical content and producers of technical content. It is indeed true that the use of Facebook, Twitter, and YouTube allows larger populations to share information through technology. However, accomplishing a simple and routine action such as posting a status update on Facebook is not the same as having deeper interest in or broader competency with technology. Such distinctions in comfort level with or knowledge about technology may affect student confidence with using novel presentation software or programs that would allow them to illustrate quantitative data, edit and embed film clips, or engage in other more advanced activities that they do not perform routinely in their daily lives. The divide has moved beyond physical access toward trends in technology usage based on cognitive ability and sociodemographic factors such as motivation and confidence. Still, like the first-level digital divide, socioeconomics has a lot to do with it: The more economically advantaged have more advanced programming skills and related communication skills, as well as more leisure time to engage with and influence how technology evolves in our society.

Asking students to raise their hands to signal ownership of a laptop is not sufficient, since having physical access to a computer does not mean having equal levels of technical expertise or appetite. Whether based on socioeconomic circumstances, age, country of origin, or even personal preference, our undergraduate students vary in terms of their technical skills and confidence. Despite what we generally perceive as *universal* access to technology, it's important to resist the temptation to think that all students enjoy equality in regard to their technical competencies. Instructors can devise ways of doing a technology inventory in the class (for example, using a survey questionnaire on the first day of class) and then move forward with a fairly comprehensive view of the range of experiences and skills.

Providing Students with the Technological Resources They Need

As we discuss throughout this book, linguistically diverse students come to class possessing varied types of preparation based on various factors (including their educational backgrounds, countries of origin, and socioeconomic circumstances). Just as they embody diversity with regard to their literacies in English and other languages, ESL and international students also possess varying levels of experience and expertise in technology. It is therefore wise for instructors to resist making assumptions about ESL and international students, and to take the time to discover to what degree students can benefit from additional skills-based training and access to other confidence-building resources. This is important because technology anxiety is inversely related to technology experience.

In some cases, even in classrooms populated by linguistically diverse students, instructors may figure out quickly that their students know more than they themselves do about technology. Or international students may be more familiar and comfortable with using open-source software rather than commercial products from Microsoft and Adobe used by most instructors in the United States. Some instructors may feel intimidated by this reality, while others may be inspired to take steps to advance their own skills. It would be beneficial for all students if they were able to see and discuss the different software their international classmates have used. In other cases, however, instructors may learn that their students need more opportunities to advance their technology skills in order to reduce their anxieties about technology and become more effective communicators.

It is important for instructors to connect students to the many resources available to our ESL and international students. Most university and college campuses, for example, have a variety of non-credit workshops available for students to learn technologies. Some university libraries host online training programs (e.g., lynda.com, howcast.com, howstuffworks.com, and SuTree.com). In most cases, these resources are equally available to instructors. YouTube also has videos on just about every how-to question pertaining to presentation software and technology. To keep students from possibly feeling overwhelmed by the amount of accessible material on YouTube, instructors should curate a playlist of video tutorials for the class to focus their learning.

ESL and international students who feel less confident in their skill level should be encouraged to consult and learn from their peers, family, or employers, and then bring these learned skills back to the communication classroom. Allowing students to work together using presentation software is another way to further enrich our diverse classrooms. Depending on the class schedule, instructors can reserve time for the class to work on their PowerPoints or other presentation aids, so that these students have guidance at hand. They should also be invited to practice their presentations using the particular technology available in the classroom, so that they can avoid any glitches and have less anxiety on presentation day.

OPPORTUNITIES AND CHALLENGES FOR USING TECHNOLOGY

Instructors of public speaking have long believed that audiences are better able to engage with speakers who use visual aids. A visual aid is anything beyond the spoken word that a speaker can use to help audiences understand a message. The creative use of visual aids can make a presentation more interesting, simplify a complex topic, and help presentations make lasting impressions.

Technology as a Visual Aid

Technology can certainly be used as a visual aid or to generate a variety of visual support for speeches. When done well, technology allows students to share images, graphs or diagrams, video, audio clips, bulleted lists, passages of text, or other visual objects. It allows students to communicate with audiences in the same room or even on the opposite side of the planet. Technology can help audiences remember complex content and can be used to save electronic and print documents to be shared later. It allows students to record presentations and to use teleconferencing technologies to present in real time over great distances. The benefits are numerous and well documented. However, as is always the case with the use of visual aids, students should analyze the rhetorical situation and select the most appropriate technology for their purposes and audiences.

For linguistically diverse students, technology can provide additional benefits, such as providing students with simultaneous translation and assisting with accent reduction. In their speaking engagements, our ESL and international students can use technology to help them clarify their messages, overcome the effect of accents, help audiences visualize unfamiliar material in support of their main points, and help them remember content. These are all part of building competent speaking skills that increase students' confidence in themselves as public speakers — and as speakers of English. Students as audience members can benefit, too. Research has long indicated that ESL students perceive instructors' use of presentation slides as aids in note taking. Technology can also augment listening comprehension and make content seem more organized and clear. Given these benefits, a thorough analysis of audience should drive students' decisions about technology. Students should be encouraged to ask: What are the audience's needs and expectations? And, of all the choices available, which technology will work best with this particular audience? The technology that students ultimately select should support the speaker's points and the audience's needs and expectations.

Challenges for Students Using Technology

The use of presentation software presents several specific challenges that instructors can incorporate into a general discussion of visual aids. For example, students should make certain that the size of the text projected on a screen is legible given the presentation setting and audience size. Students should also be warned that the consequences of errors in spelling or grammar that appear in presentation slides are amplified by being projected on large screens, making proofreading even more necessary as part of the revision process. Having text-heavy slides that almost function as manuscripts of speech content is another common mistake presenters make.

It is also important for our students to remember that like language-based communication, visual communication is culturally specific. Diagrams, symbols, and signs shared through technology can mean one thing to audiences in one culture and something else to audiences in a different culture. In a public speaking course that includes linguistically diverse students, instructors should dedicate adequate class time to the topic of visual rhetoric. Students should explore how drawings, diagrams, photos, and charts can help speakers explain content and ideas to some audience members, and at the same time, might confuse others. The extraordinary work done by the International Organization for Standardization, displayed in signage in airports around the world, can be used as exemplars to illustrate clear messaging across international audiences in ways that overcome cultural and other types of biases.

In addition to encouraging students to study the cultural aspects of visual communication, instructors also should raise awareness of other common pitfalls associated with students learning how to use technology effectively in the public speaking classroom. For example, researchers note that new technologies can tempt students to be underprepared for classroom presentations. That is, some students, when being introduced to new skills, spend too much time learning and preparing the technology and not enough time researching and preparing their content or practicing their delivery. On a related matter, some students mistakenly substitute the quantity of presentation slides for the quality of the content being delivered. It is always more important to have something to say than to just say a lot.

Planning for the Unexpected

Finally, students often fail to fully recognize the risk of technology glitches such as power failures, failed Internet connections, incompatible versions of software, and other surprises that can railroad an otherwise well-prepared presentation. Technology can fail just when speakers need it the most. Though the lesson is usually not fully learned by students until they are faced with an obstacle like this, we should encourage students to be prepared for anything to happen, to have a solid backup plan, and to be ready to present their work at any time with no technology at all. To prepare for these circumstances, it is important for instructors to provide opportunities for students to practice, including rehearsing presentations in the setting and with the same equipment in which their speeches will be delivered. Practice sessions also can be set aside in which students are forced to present without technology and other visual aids.

BACK TO THE BASICS: FOUNDATIONAL PRIORITIES IN PUBLIC SPEAKING

In the 1990s, there were several well-publicized backlashes against what was perceived by many as the overuse of technology in professional presentations. High-profile leaders of the U.S. military and in Fortune 500 companies publicly blamed the proliferation of presentation software for ineffective public speaking. Army generals expressed concern over national security, saying that their subordinates were spending too much time searching for the latest template, and warned of severe consequences if speakers failed to keep their presentations on task and to the point. Their criticism, though extreme, remains somewhat relevant today. Students would be wise to resist temptations to dazzle their instructors with the latest technologies and instead focus diligently on substance.

For students in the process of learning new technologies, who have not yet gained the necessary skills or confidence, going "old school" with their selection of visual aids can be an option, especially in an introductory public speaking course. Using a marker board or sharing a print photograph can be highly effective, keeping the audience focused on the speaker rather than staring at slide after slide from a popular template. In many ways, simple options can often be the best choices, and a speaker can stand out by using a flip chart — a large pad of paper on an easel-like stand. Pages can be prepared with text in advance or used by speakers during the presentation itself to draw, outline, or create a list. The advantages and disadvantages of these old-school approaches should be discussed along with those associated with technology.

Technology works best when it is used to help audiences quickly grasp what is being shared and then returns the focus to the speaker. If audiences are forced to stare at the projection screen or down at printed handouts, students risk losing connection with their audiences. Technology can help students make their points understandable to diverse audiences. However, they should be reminded that the speaker, not the technology, should always be the center of attention. As is always the case, students should use technology to share their ideas and perspectives, and should not allow the technology itself to be the center of attention or overly rely on it for their assigned tasks.

In the introductory public speaking classroom, we recommend asking students to skip technology entirely at first. Students should begin with showing a strong understanding of the subject matter, analyzing their audiences and understanding their norms and expectations, and discovering what is customary for various types of presentations. Then, when presentation software is allowed in later speech assignments, students should not overdo technology. They should use simple layouts, test their visuals for cultural biases, and seek feedback from their peers, their instructor, and specialists on the content being presented. They should remember that while something might be clear to one person, including the speaker, it may not be clear to another.

Public speaking is about sharing our ideas and our concerns with others and offering insights and perspectives on a topic that is important to us. Our goal is to present clear, accurate information, focusing on the specific needs of our audience and a specific set of purposes. Once the foundations have been established, technology might very well be a useful tool to help us meet our goals.

Whether students are communicating face-to-face, in a live performance mediated by technology, or through a prerecorded presentation integrated to a Web site or transmitted as a file through email, the focus should be on them as speakers, on their message, and on the authentic connections they can make to their audiences. For our introductory-level students, it is their primary responsibility to know their material, organize it effectively, be prepared, and understand their audience. Speakers should then use technology judiciously to support the task, remembering to keep things simple and clear. Students must understand that technology supports the speech; the speech does not support the technology.

CLASSROOM ACTIVITIES

As a self-reflection exercise, ask students to conduct an inventory of their current technology skills. How do they typically learn how to use a new technology? Beyond the basic instruction on technology offered in the public speaking course, how can they advance their technology skills to support their presentations?

Ask students to research resources on campus, off campus, and online that they can utilize to develop these important skills. Have them report back and collect the various resources into a common listing to distribute to the class.

As an assignment other than a speech, ask students to do an interview with someone in a profession they may be interested in pursuing, asking them about the kinds of presentations the person is required to give and how technology is used in those presentations. Have students share some of the main points in class discussion.

In a large-group discussion, ask students to list ten reasons why they should use technology to enhance a presentation for an upcoming assignment. Then, in individual reflections, ask the students to think about what specific kinds of technology they *can* use and *should* use, given their current skill set, their personal goals, their audience's needs, and the instructor's expectations. Encourage students to consider among their many options "old school" technologies (e.g., flip charts) and justify their decisions.

Ask students to imagine that they have been given an assignment to create a short presentation on the topic of selecting a major. Their audience is made up of high school seniors who plan to attend your college or university next year. What kinds of technology might be most appropriate and effective for this task? Ask the students in what ways the task would be different if the high school seniors were all international students, reflecting on content, visuals, format, and other relevant matters.

As a homework assignment, ask students to prepare a one-minute presentation to be delivered in class. During the next class meeting, tell them to pretend that the power went out in the room where they were scheduled to present. Dim the lights and ask them to take turns delivering their one-minute presentation, using only their voices. Challenge them to communicate effectively and engage their audience without using any technology, gestures, eye contact, or facial expressions. Afterward, have the students reflect about the opportunities and challenges of this task. Discuss the importance of preparing for the unexpected.

Ask students to plan a presentation about your campus for an overseas audience of business professionals. Have them reflect about the opportunities and challenges of this task. Have them formulate a backup plan so that they are able to deliver the presentation even if technical limitations of the host country prevent them from using presentation software and budget constraints prevent their use of printed handouts.

8

The Community-Engaged Public Speaking Course

Since the early 1990s, interest in community-based teaching and learning has proliferated across the discipline of communication and its various subfields. A course on public speaking is a natural fit for service-learning pedagogy, given our focus on civic discourse and the vast range of topics about which our students speak. Adding a service-learning assignment to a public speaking course or integrating a course with a community partnership can create a vibrant learning opportunity for students, as well as result in positive consequences for the community. We introduce a variety of ways to incorporate community-based learning into the public speaking course, including those that are relatively straightforward to implement.

Community-based projects benefit all students by introducing them to new ideas and experiences, heightening their commitment to speaking effectively to a variety of audiences, and helping them understand and improve their pragmatic communicative skills. Research suggests that nontraditional college students may benefit the most from these experiences. That is, first-generation students, low-income students, and students from historically underrepresented groups show stronger learning gains from high-impact learning practices like community-based learning.

These types of projects additionally enhance ESL students' understanding of the linguistic features of English, support their growth in cultural knowledge and literacies, and provide a setting outside the traditional classroom in which they can practice their English. An increasing number of public speaking sections on many campuses now include some sort of community-based learning component or approach. It is important to anticipate that community-engaged learning may be perceived and embraced differently by linguistically and culturally diverse students in your course.

This chapter begins with a cursory introduction to the rationale for community-based learning and a brisk overview of the keys to effective service learning, though the scope and specific purpose of this book prevents us from offering too much detail on these topics. Rather, we focus on the particular issues you may face with a linguistically and culturally diverse student group, and we propose some solutions to help turn these challenges into productive learning opportunities in your public speaking course. In this broad overview, the terms community-based learning and service learning will be used more or less interchangeably.

CIVIC AND COMMUNITY ENGAGEMENT IN PUBLIC SPEAKING COURSES

Arising from a call for higher education to promote civic engagement, the service-learning movement is now maturing as an academic field. Broadly understood, service learning involves the integration of disciplinary content with deliberate civic learning, grounded in and informed by a community-based learning experience and amplified by individual and collective critical reflection. Research shows that service learning facilitates both cognitive and applied learning outcomes, and enhances both disciplinary and general student learning. Regardless of the discipline in which it is employed, service learning helps students gain a deeper understanding of their world as an interdependent system and improves their diversity, civic, and global awareness. Compatible with the aims of the public speaking course, then, service learning nurtures student knowledge about their civic rights and responsibilities and creates opportunities for students to learn *in situ* about social issues.

Effective Community Engagement

In order to ensure that a service-learning experience is effective for student learning and worthwhile for our community partners, a number of key elements should be considered. It is important to select appropriate community-based learning experiences that match the goals of the course and serve the genuine needs and interests of the community. Most campuses have offices and dedicated staff to support community-based learning and student volunteerism. These professional colleagues can guide faculty to community agencies and organizations that already have relationships with your campus and can assist in preparing students for immersion into the community, which is particularly important to effective community engagement and diversity learning. The most effective and sustainable community partnerships are based on mutuality of benefits and allow for collaboration in design of projects and assignments.

While civic learning is a central element of most public speaking courses and will not require much extra thought, the integration of critical reflection activities may require special attention. Ensuring that students have opportunities to share their community-based learning experiences with their classmates and provide written reflection on their community-based learning will reinforce the benefits of service-learning pedagogy and support more integrative student learning. Students need opportunities to analyze, synthesize, and evaluate what they have learned in and through their service experience, as well as from the agency personnel and others in the community who should be seen as co-educators. Some classroom activities and reflective writing assignments are suggested at the end of this chapter to help guide you in this process.

Obviously, this introduction is not, by itself, sufficient preparation for someone who aims to teach a service-learning course for the first time. There are many elements to plan, logistical issues to work out in coordination with community partners, and ethical dilemmas to consider prior to adopting service-learning pedagogy. We recommend that faculty read the literature on community-based teaching and learning prior to planning any related assignments or activities, and we suggest some useful sources in the annotated bibliography at the end of this text. Each instructor also should assess the value of community-engaged assignments to the public speaking students in their courses and to the community agencies or partners in their geographic region. At various points in the process, faculty should work closely with agency personnel to evaluate the benefits of this pedagogical approach to the community being served.

Community-Engaged Speeches

Public speaking courses can use a variety of approaches for integrating community-based learning components. This section offers some common examples. Subsequent sections of this chapter will consider issues and adaptations that might support more linguistically and culturally diverse student needs.

Generally, there are three typical categories of presentations in the public speaking classroom that map to service learning: speaking *about* a community agency and/or the issues it addresses based on a service experience; speaking *on behalf of* a community agency or partner organization as a form of community service; and speaking to the class *about the service experience itself* on a topic informed by that experience.

To elaborate, one common approach asks students to choose an organization in which they can do some specified amount of community service and to speak about the organization to the class. Typically working with the campus office that matches students to volunteer service opportunities, students can propose community engagements that will inform their presentations. As they learn about the organization and its work, coupled with some additional research, they present descriptive or informative speeches; this approach could be adapted to fit a typical persuasive speaking assignment as well, where the student advocates for attitude or policy change. One benefit of this approach is that it moves students off campus and out into the community. Virtually any type of agency and any type of service can be relevant to this assignment. The collection of speeches forms a broad consciousness-raising opportunity for students in the class. Through each other's speeches they become aware of community issues and organizations that link their local area to the broader challenges of the day. They also learn about volunteer opportunities, which may precipitate subsequent community engagement. Students often report that even these relatively low-impact service engagements push them outside their comfort zones, open them to new ideas and experiences, and heighten their commitment to speaking effectively. The range of social issues and of community organizations that address them also provides a broad context for students to understand the world around them and to consider sites where dedicated professionals and informed citizens seek positive social change.

Another common approach is for students to speak on behalf of community agencies. To prepare for this task, the students become trained to serve on the speaker's bureau or outreach team for a community organization (rather than providing direct service to clients), helping to get the message out to the larger community. In this approach, students can practice their public speaking skills for the benefit of the community, while also learning about the organization and its mission, its relationship to different audiences, and the challenges many nonprofit organizations face in building community awareness and involvement. In a related example, public speaking students can form their own speaker's bureau to, for instance, speak to under-resourced local middle and high school students about aspects of college life: deciding how to select a college, developing effective college applications, choosing a major, and so forth. This approach can provide a simple but valuable service to schools and their pupils and can also give your students good public speaking practice. Such an assignment, and subsequent reflection on it, invites college students to consider their relative privilege and related tacit knowledge specifically in relation to higher education.

The third approach is for students to speak to the class about the service experience itself. This process may begin with students spending a number of weeks doing direct service under the supervision of a community organization such as a homeless shelter or Head Start program. Such engagements often require extensive training for students, preparing them to engage deeply with client populations, and therefore may not be suitable for courses offered on the quarter system or in accelerated formats. During a full semester, however, students could potentially serve for eight to ten weeks, allowing ample time for pre-immersion preparation. These service-learning experiences provide opportunities, for example, to give informative speeches about the experience of serving specific populations, demonstration speeches about one of the central activities related to the agency that might focus more substantively on day-to-day interface with client populations or on-the-ground work, or persuasive speeches that connect scholarly research about an issue that their service site addresses to a policy debate. These speeches go deeper than those described in the first example, because students spend a considerable amount of time sharing details of their own experience rather than more introductory information about issues and agencies. Speeches informed by longer-term and deeper immersion in the community tend to be infused with ethos and pathos gained through the service experience that strengthens the quality of speeches. More advanced public speaking courses focused on argumentation, advocacy, and deliberative dialogue also can be significantly enhanced through employing community-based learning.

Many variations on these assignments are possible; the main point is that community-based learning can employ shorter-term or longer-term service immersions and can provide the basis for a variety of speech assignments. The remainder of this chapter turns the focus to leveraging the cultural and linguistic diversity of the classroom for public speaking courses using community-engaged teaching models and learning experiences.

CHALLENGES AND OPPORTUNITIES FOR LINGUISTICALLY DIVERSE STUDENTS

If you imagine a typical service-learning course in the United States, as many critics have done, you may picture a white middle- or upper-middle-class college student engaged with agencies that serve poor, minority, and immigrant populations. However, given the growing diversity of the U.S. college classroom, and the growing complexity of our multicultural society, these stereotypes of college students and community service no longer hold true.

Nevertheless, despite its growing acceptance as a pedagogical approach across disciplines, some ESL and international students may perceive an array of challenges with regard to community-based learning opportunities. Some of these challenges will be logistical, such as lack of familiarity with the array of nonprofit organizations and the availability of transportation. As mentioned before, working with campus community service offices can help you overcome most logistical barriers. However, instructors also must help the staff in those offices understand the specific needs and perspectives of international and ESL students when it comes to community service, just as it is helpful to be in dialogue with these staff about assignment design and community partnership development to ensure effective learning experiences for your students. Offices that serve international students on your campus also can be helpful in this regard.

It is important to remember that among the international and ESL students we might find in our classes are a large number of non–traditional-aged students. They may have multiple responsibilities beyond school, including part- or full-time employment, responsibilities to families of origin here or at home, as well as to their own spouses and children, within their religious organizational affiliations, and so forth. As much as possible, you should encourage students to propose service experiences or other types of community-based learning that dovetail with their full range of responsibilities while still meeting assignment criteria. Such an approach encourages students to see academic learning, community service, and routine daily life in an integrated way.

Pointing students to the benefits of community-based learning can balance out what may be initially perceived as inconveniences. Current research demonstrates that traditionally underrepresented college students, including first-generation students and those from minority populations or low-income backgrounds, experience even greater benefits from high-impact learning experiences (like service learning) than do students from majority populations. Similarly, while most classroom-based experiences focus on improving ESL students' understanding of the linguistic features of English, informal settings that are more social and dynamic in nature, such as volunteer sites, help students understand and improve their pragmatic communicative skills. Community-based learning is known to develop the language ability of ESL students by providing another environment in which to practice their English. It also supports growth in students' cultural knowledge and communicative fluency. This may also apply to international students who are bilingual or to non-native speakers of standard American English. Even domestic students from divergent regions of the country who want to become more familiar with the dialects, colloquialisms, and social dynamics of diverse U.S. contexts can benefit from community-based learning. However, while gaining insight into the breadth of American culture and social issues is an invaluable learning experience for all students, some research has shown that poorly designed community service can actually reinforce, rather than disrupt, prejudice and stereotypes, so faculty must be quite intentional in structuring learning and reflection activities that work against this negative outcome.

Community service has been shown to aid in the cross-cultural adjustment of international students, who build more complex networks in the host culture by engaging more deeply in off-campus environments, with a wider range of local people. Community partner organizations provide contexts where international and ESL students can volunteer; such organizations can meet a variety of students' disciplinary interests, as well as their career goals, social and political orientations, language abilities, and service sensibilities (e.g., direct service with client populations, office support, or physical labor).

On the other hand, some ESL students may prefer to serve in contexts using their native language, even while they prepare and deliver their assigned speeches in English. We believe this is something faculty should support, particularly because our primary purpose is not English language instruction. Service in this type of setting helps connect students to their home cultures, can alleviate feelings of loneliness that often accompany study-abroad or immigration experiences, and may assist with students' integration of the longer-term changes they experience as an outcome of extended cultural immersion. Such engagements are additionally a wonderful way for organizations that serve ethnic enclave communities to experience productive interface with your university and come to see the campus as an ally in their work.

Reflecting on Cultural Meanings of Service and Civic Engagement

We cannot assume that community service has equivalent meanings across all cultures, or that it is valued in equivalent ways. In some cultures, volunteering through nonprofit organizations may be unusual because service to the community is so embedded within quotidian life through kinship networks and close neighborhood geographies. Given the wide range of political systems in the world, contemporary educational notions of civic engagement may or may not resonate with all students. Reflecting on the dynamics of power and privilege that imbue all service-learning and community-based education projects is important. This process involves a consideration of the diversity of our students and of the belief systems and experiences they carry into service engagements. It behooves us to consider how notions of service are culturally and linguistically constructed and how these issues may involve complex intersections of language, race, ethnicity, class, gender, sexuality, ability, and country of origin.

International students, particularly at many elite colleges and universities that do not offer financial aid to international students, may come from relatively affluent backgrounds in their home countries. Some ESL or fully bilingual students may be among the many undocumented students who were brought to the United States as children or adolescents and have succeeded in public education and now find themselves in college. Others may have migrated as children with professional parents who are among the most educated and well-paid in the U.S. workforce. Some students may have come to the United States, whether permanently or just for their college education, under very difficult circumstances, such as through political sanctuary movements, and may have had little formal study of English prior to migration. Others may be studying in the United States for only a semester or a year, with widely varying English competencies, before returning to their home countries and campuses. These are only a few examples of the many backgrounds our culturally and linguistically diverse students may bring to a service-learning assignment.

Such factors should be kept in mind, as they may affect students' attitudes about or experiences with nonprofit organizations. Undocumented students, for example, may worry that proof of citizenship or background checks might be required and may not feel comfortable disclosing this concern to their instructors. Indeed, in organizations that serve children, fingerprinting and sometimes extensive background checks are usually required. For campuses in complex urban environments, some of our students may be (or have been) among the clients served by community partner organizations, and this could create a sense of awkwardness or embarrassment for them. On the other hand, such students may welcome the opportunity to "give back" to an agency that has been instrumental in their own well-being and road to education.

CREATING EFFECTIVE COMMUNITY-BASED ASSIGNMENTS

Faculty routinely give a good deal of thought to the structure of their assignments in relation to their overall course learning goals. With community-based teaching and service-learning pedagogy, another layer of thought will be required, but there are many resources available through Campus Compact and other organizations to help with this process.

Working with Community Partners

One best practice is to develop a set of partnerships and work with them over a period of time and across multiple sections of a public speaking course. Some departments develop long-standing partnerships that are multifaceted and mutually beneficial. In these cases, faculty and agency personnel can share ideas about assignments to ensure that student-learning goals map well to agency needs and that the partner organizations have sufficient resources (i.e., personnel, time, sites) to support students. University staff will be a frontline resource for brainstorming, developing, and troubleshooting service-learning courses and student experiences.

Leveraging Linguistic Diversity

While faculty may initially find that the linguistic diversity of their public speaking course poses challenges, it is also a tremendous asset for community-based learning. In most areas of the country, cultural enclaves and associated organizations provide a matrix of community engagement opportunities for our students. For example, a few courses at our university partner with an organization that supports victims of human trafficking. There are many aspects to the work, often involving a wide variety of language needs. Students' native languages can be quite useful to such organizations, whether for translation, interactions with families, providing support for victims, or helping with research. For more commonly spoken languages in our geographic region, like Spanish, Portuguese, Greek, and Russian, there are dozens of organizations supporting large and complex communities of first-, second-, and third-generation populations across domains as varied as education, social services, legal aid, health care, and business. Students who struggle with some aspects of English or more general aspects of public speaking may build confidence by providing a useful service in their native language.

Tailoring Assignments to Diverse Student Classrooms

As we have discussed throughout this book, public speaking courses are likely to have diverse students enrolled, including domestic and international students with many linguistic and cultural backgrounds. This diversity may require a thoughtful and flexible approach to assignments. For example, we have encountered religious students who prefer to serve only in their own faith communities and others who have protested the service experiences or views of fellow students due to political disagreement. We have had students express concerns about their safety going to and from community service placements, whether based on entrenched stereotypes about the inner city or due to concrete realities concerning crime rates and difficult transportation routes. In developing a community-based component for your public speaking course, when such concerns are raised, you could allow students to partner with one another, or work in small groups for their service experiences. This may additionally help build their confidence or alleviate their fears, while also allaying some parental concerns. Overall, open conversation with students, listening to individual and collective students' concerns and preferences, and engaging productively with appropriate campus staff and community partner organization personnel can help alleviate many concerns and identify workable solutions.

Alternative Assignments and Risk Management

In many ways, community-engaged learning involves what can be understood as risks. For overscheduled and already stressed-out students, service commitments bring additional schedule challenges that, in turn, can create additional stress. Community service experiences may have psycho-emotional effects and political impacts on students as they confront inequities and injustices and observe situations they may find shocking or upsetting. While holistic learning is one of the main benefits of service learning, students may be upset by what they routinely encounter, witness, or learn through their service experiences. Faculty should ensure that appropriate campus staff are aware of when and where their students are embedded in the community, and should consult with academic leaders about appropriate waivers and related paperwork that students might be asked to provide.

For these and similar reasons, alternative assignments should be made available. For example, students without cars or without access to public transportation, students whose schedules are truly intractable (as is often the case for science and engineering students or student athletes), or students whose cultural or political beliefs are prohibitive might engage with a campus-based organization or club instead of a local nonprofit organization. Students can learn about the mission of a campus organization, engage in activities it organizes for the benefit of others, and share their experience in a speech about the organization and the broader issues it seeks to address. We have included an assignment like this for first-year students early in the semester as a way to facilitate their initial engagement beyond their academic program and residence hall. In more particular cases, for a female Muslim student whose parents forbade community service and for a wheelchair-bound student whose disability made off-campus service too onerous, alternative assignments were arranged.

Finally, there are also risks to the faculty members who choose community-based teaching and learning, and we would be remiss not to mention some of them. Despite the growing popularity of service-learning pedagogy, colleagues may not understand or sufficiently value community-based teaching and learning in the discipline. This can put contingently employed (i.e., pre-tenure, adjunct, or term) faculty at risk professionally. A more mundane though not insignificant risk involves the time required to facilitate quality community-based learning within sustainable community partnerships. Nevertheless, despite such risks, few teaching approaches provide as deep a sense of satisfaction while also producing potentially transformational learning for our students and a multitude of potential benefits within our communities. For us, the opportunity to integrate our teaching with community-based research and the scholarship of teaching and learning (SoTL) has been both professionally productive and personally rewarding.

CLASSROOM ACTIVITIES

In the large-group setting, ask students to define what the term *community service* means to them. Then pair students to share a prior community service experience they have had. Give them a set of questions to address with each other, such as why they chose to serve, what the agency or organization does for the community, what language and culture issues they encountered, and what they learned about the community and themselves in the process. Ask them how they have previously shared that experience with others through interpersonal or public communication. For students who have never experienced community service, for whatever reason, ask them to describe a local, national, or international nonprofit organization that they respect or admire and to answer similar questions about it.

Ask students to make a list of activities that they consider *civic engagement* (we recommend using or adapting the exercise on civic engagement described in Howard's workbook, listed in the annotated bibliography. We add an item to the list on speaking about issues of public importance to friends or on campus). This activity can function as an icebreaker in addition to helping students explore divergent notions of service and civic duty. Facilitate a discussion that teases out the reasons for this diversity of opinions and invites students to share their own examples. This exercise can be useful even without having a service-learning component in order to explore students' cultural variations in understandings of civic responsibility and the role of public discourse.

Invite a representative of a community-based organization to visit your class to share the many kinds of public speaking she or he routinely does on behalf of the organization. Encourage the students to apply course concepts from the textbook in their questions to the representative (e.g., "How do you establish your credibility with audiences?"). Ask the representative to share examples of how linguistic and cultural diversity impacts their speaking engagements.

Invite staff from the office of international programs, community service office, office of service learning, or similar unit on your campus to help orient students in advance of their community engagements. Ensure they include discussion of cultural and linguistic diversity.

Several times during the semester, design a brief exercise through which students are prompted to write some reflections on their community service experiences in relation to concepts from the textbook, and also in relation to their diversity learning and civic learning. Vary how students share these reflections (e.g., "write, pair, share," small-group discussions, whole class discussion, or turning in reflections as journal entries). Move from ungraded short reflections to longer graded critical essays that might also serve as metacognitive evaluations of their speeches and learning.

If community-engaged components will not work in your class, do an exercise where students imagine giving their speech to a variety of audiences associated with community service and civic engagement. Ask them to consider cultural and linguistic factors related to themselves, the settings, the audiences, and the issues.

Conclusion

We hope *ESL Students in the Public Speaking Classroom* helps you anticipate and address some of the particularities related to teaching public speaking in culturally and linguistically diverse classrooms. In these eight chapters, we have covered some of the most fundamental concerns: the profile and diversity of ESL students, cultural variability in classroom interaction patterns and learning styles, specific linguistic concerns for public speaking instruction, special notes for helping ESL students plan and practice their speeches, and some key concerns regarding extemporaneous speech delivery.

Our goals have been twofold. First, we wanted instructors to understand the needs of their international, ESL, and other non-native English-speaking students—needs that arise from both linguistic and cultural factors that are part of complex and varied personal and social histories. Second, and perhaps more important, we hoped to prompt a valuable discussion about cultural diversity in the public speaking classroom. Recalling that speech is the unique domain of human beings, and public discourse is the primary means of enacting civil society, it seems imperative that questions and practices of intercultural understanding enter into the beginning public speaking course.

We hope we struck a balance between exploring group-based linguistic and cultural identities and their shared norms and disrupting overgeneralized notions of cultural identity that assume members of national or ethnic groups necessarily share such norms. Technology and globalization, decades of multiculturalism, and youth orientations to identity have, in fact, led to myriad blendings, hybridities, and individualisms that may belie some of the traditional ethnographic sense of cultural cohesion. Additionally, course instructors who are non-native speakers of Standard American English will bring perspectives and experiences that may contradict and deeply enrich the discussion in this book. International graduate students, instructors with recent immigrant histories (first- or second-generation), those who have studied other languages and/or lived abroad for extended periods of time, those who have created multicultural families and live daily in negotiations of divergent norms and behaviors, and those from nondominant U.S. heritage who have developed "outsider-within" perspectives all will be differently situated in the college classroom and uniquely capable of adding much to this discussion.

We hope the array of cultural perspectives, specific instructional strategies, assignment ideas, and resources for future reading that we have introduced may enrich your teaching in other subject areas and provide the basis for rich dialogues about teaching with your colleagues. In our experience, communication instructors are among the most dedicated to the teaching enterprise and to student empowerment in the contemporary university. As such, many communication faculty commit to the scholarship of teaching and learning (SoTL) within their overall research agendas. While it was not a primary goal of this book, we hope we also have introduced potential research topics and resources that will support those interests.

We wish you all the luck in your teaching activities, and we hope your diverse classroom is exciting, enriching, and empowering for you and your students!

Selected Scholarship: A Bibliography

This book is based on research and scholarship published across many areas of communication studies, linguistics, and education pedagogy. While engaging deeply in scholarly debates is not a primary goal for a book like this, we know that many instructors will appreciate having a list of additional resources and will take the opportunity to read more on the subjects that inform this book. Therefore, we have provided as an appendix a list of some key sources related to the topic. This bibliography does not provide a comprehensive overview of every important scholarly contribution to the field. Rather, it is intended as a starting point for teachers of public speaking who wish to expand their familiarity with previously published research. This bibliography provides an initial road map to further reading.

The topics covered in each of our chapters relate to entire fields of inquiry in a variety of areas of communication studies, linguistics, TESOL, and pedagogical theory and practice. Given our specific purpose, then, we focus here on sources specifically related to working with linguistically diverse students in the public speaking classroom. The bibliographic citations are followed immediately by brief annotations that summarize the topics covered. In addition, most of the works mentioned here include extensive reference lists specific to their subjects or are part of useful anthologies on related topics. We hope that these references can lead you to a deeper understanding of a challenge you currently face in your classroom or academic program, or that they provide you with the beginnings of a foundation you need for an action-research project you plan to undertake to inform your scholarship of teaching and learning.

Archer, D. (1997). Unspoken diversity: Cultural differences in gestures. *Qualitative Sociology*, *20*(1), 79–105.

> The author points out that gestures as a form of nonverbal communication are not universally understood. The article explores how one acquires gestures and describes the profound differences in hand gestures across cultures. Archer promotes "gestural humility" (i.e., assuming that our gestures may be interpreted incorrectly by audiences from other cultures). He concludes with a description of nuanced behaviors and an analysis of cultural meta-differences in performing and comprehending gestures.

Braithwaite, C. A., & Braithwaite, D. O. (1991). Instructional communication strategies for adapting to a multicultural introductory course. *Basic Communication Course Annual*, *3*, 145–160.

> The authors propose that instructors use an ethnographic approach in order to adapt teaching practices to increasingly diverse classroom settings. Strategies are offered in regard to presenting students with a "problematic" understanding of culture to heighten students' awareness of differences and similarities. The authors offer

assignments that encourage students to reflect on their own cultural patterns of communication and offer several resources instructors might use to explore multicultural dimensions of the public speaking classroom.

Campus Compact, compact.org

Campus Compact, founded in 1985, is a consortium of over 1,000 colleges and universities in the United States forged by their presidents to promote and support the civic purpose of higher education. Dedicated to promoting public and community awareness among students and helping educators teach civic skills and social responsibility, Campus Compact provides instructional resources for curricular infusion of citizenship education, community-based learning, and campus-community partnership development. Campus Compact has led the service-learning movement. Its Web page houses a variety of resources, including syllabi across disciplines and institutions that illustrate how to incorporate service-learning and community engagement; specific syllabi in "communications" relevant to public speaking classes include those for effective oral communication, persuasion, and speech.

Cyphert, D. (2002). Public speaking in a second language. In J. S. Trent (Ed.), *Included in communication: Learning climates that cultivate racial and ethnic diversity* (pp. 141–148). Washington, D.C.: AAHE/NCA.

The author summarizes challenges faced by students making presentations in their second language to audiences who lack familiarity with the speaker's culture, native language, and communication practices. Cyphert suggests (1) introducing students in cross-cultural public speaking classes to issues of linguistic dissimilarity as part of the curriculum and (2) emphasizing that learning to be an engaged audience member in a complex rhetorical setting is part of living and working in a diverse society. A series of strategies are offered to help speakers and audiences prepare for communication interactions with a focus on comprehension rather than native-like command of the English language. The advice for instructors includes suggestions for classroom activities and assessment of student learning.

Dick, R. C. (1990). A case for exclusive sections of the basic oral communication course: International ESL students. *ACA Bulletin, 73,* 39–44.

As a "proposition of principle," the author recommends that special sections of public speaking courses be designed for international students who speak English as their second language. Dick points to the issue of student "noninvolvement" as a primary motivating factor and compares mixed classes to expecting ESL students to "enter a footrace while they are learning to walk." He warns instructors that excessive pressure to conform may lead ESL students to withdraw, and he points out that in his observations, many instructors unfairly hesitate to call on ESL students during class discussions. To support his argument, Dick also quotes other instructors at his institution who worried that ESL students would not be able to compete with students who were native English speakers and, therefore, would be better served in special sections. Though views on this issue have changed over time, this article reflects common perceptions of researchers, scholars, and teachers in the late 1980s, at which time there was less optimism about ESL and international students' ability to mesh with U.S. students.

Downing, J., & Garmon, C. (2001). Teaching students in the basic course how to use presentation software. *Communication Education, 50*(3), 218–229.

The authors report the positive impact on students' confidence resulting from their receiving training in the effective use of technology in presentations. In summarizing previous research, the authors point out that ESL students particularly appreciate speakers' use of presentation software, including instructors' use of it in academic settings. Downing and Garmon point out that while using technology to aid communication effectiveness remains a necessary workplace competency, especially in but not limited to culturally diverse settings, it is also important for students to receive relevant training via instructional materials or hands-on tutelage.

Droge, D., & Ortega, B. (Eds.). (1999). *Voices of strong democracy: Concepts and models for service-learning in communication studies*. Washington, D.C.: AAHE/NCA.

This edited collection includes two brief but useful chapters that focus on the integration of community-based engagement with the public speaking classroom: one by Mark A. Pollock ("Advocacy in Service of Others: Service-Learning in Argumentation Courses," pp. 111–117) and the other by Sara Weintraub ("Giving Students 'All of the Above': Combining Service-Learning with the Public Speaking Course," pp. 119–124). Pollock summarizes reasons to incorporate community-based projects into introductory communication courses, reviews some ethical issues to consider when doing so, and offers sample assignments. Weintraub explores specific benefits to students who participate in these sorts of course enhancements, such as opportunities to instill in them a sense of responsibility towards others in society. The volume was published in the American Association for Higher Education's series on service learning in the disciplines and includes chapters related to a variety of other communication courses and subject areas.

Dudley, L. (2007). Integrating volunteering into the adult immigrant second language experience. *The Canadian Modern Language Review, 63*(4), 539–561.

To help adult immigrants learn English, the author recommends that college instructors add out-of-classroom experiences to the ESL curriculum in order to intensify language development and social integration. Dudley provides recommendations to help instructors integrate volunteer work at English-speaking organizations, a strategy intended to help students gain a more complex understanding of both the linguistic nature of language and the social nature of language learning.

Ferris, D. (1998). Students' views of academic aural/oral skills: A comparative needs analysis. *TESOL Quarterly, 32*(2), 289–318.

The author suggests that the focus of ESL instruction be expanded beyond diction, enunciation, and articulation to broader skills associated with listening comprehension and note taking. She points out that instructors and students often do not agree on the relative importance of these language skills, nor do they always share the same learning priorities. The author suggests that instructors increase their focus on helping ESL students gain more advanced abilities related to effective participation in group discussions and debates—skills associated with participation—rather than merely focusing on skills related to presentations.

Ferris, D., & Tagg, T. (1996). Academic listening/speaking tasks for ESL students: Problems, suggestions, and implications. *TESOL Quarterly, 30*(2), 297–320.

The authors investigated instructors' views on the challenges faced by ESL students in regard to a variety of listening and speaking tasks. The results indicate that many ESL students face difficulties with general listening comprehension, which leads to

challenges in lecture comprehension. The authors recommend that highly motivated ESL students be assigned to listen to sample lectures by a variety of speakers in
order to increase their opportunities to succeed in higher education. Ferris and Tagg
also recommend that training be offered to instructors who teach ESL students so
that, without oversimplifying the curriculum, they are better prepared to lecture to
linguistically diverse audiences, offer culturally accessible examples to support course
content, and manage audience questions more effectively.

Hao, R. N. (2010). (Re)Constructing ELL and international student identities in the oral
communication course. *Basic Communication Course Annual, 22*, 125–152.

The author reminds public speaking instructors that not all ESL and international
students have a low level of English proficiency, nor are they all "at risk" in the U.S.
academic setting. Hao explores how overly hasty identity constructions can prevent
ESL students from gaining acceptance and credibility in the public speaking classroom by labeling them "at risk." Doing so can result in instructors' unintentionally
creating an unwelcoming learning environment and missing out on the many ways
ESL and international students can enhance the classroom with their presence and
full participation. Hao provides a useful caution for well-intentioned instructors who
sometimes fall back on stereotypes of ESL students as special populations who have
difficulties with giving oral reports, participating in discussions, taking lecture notes,
and adapting socially. The authors recommend that instructors listen to the needs of
their students, adapt their teaching styles in order to serve the diverse student body,
resist the temptation to label ESL and international students as deficient, and work
toward making all students feel welcome and included.

Harter, L. M., Kirby, E. L., Hatfield, K. L., & Kuhlman, K. N. (2004). Spectators of public
affairs to agents of social change: Engaging students in the basic course through
service-learning. *Basic Communication Course Annual, 16*, 165–194.

The authors offer a justification for adding a service-learning component to a public
speaking course in order to combat increasingly materialistic influences, enhance the
rigor of the learning experience, and provide a meaningful service to society. Examples
of individual and collaborative assignments are offered along with strategies to engage students at the interpersonal level and troubleshoot problems that can occur.
While this article does not address particular opportunities or challenges related to
linguistically diverse student populations, the discussion of the value of engaging
with community partners is relevant.

Hendrix, K. G. (2000). Assessment and skill development for ESL students in mainstream
communication classes requiring oral presentations. *Journal of the Association for Communication Administration, 29*, 196–212.

The author offers strategies to "mainstream" instructors, those without prior training in ESL but who teach public speaking in classrooms with increasingly diverse
students. Her rhetoric-based teaching assessment and instructional strategies are
grounded in the research literature and focus on collaboration and fairness. Hendrix
reminds readers that in addition to the help we offer ESL and international students,
we should not overlook native-speaking Americans from impoverished public schools,
who also benefit from additional assistance. While the case study offered in this article is somewhat narrow in scope, the literature review and the assessment and instructional strategies are informed and useful.

Honour, D. (2007). Speech performance anxiety for non-native speakers. *The Florida Communication Journal, 35*(2), 57–66.

The author discusses communication apprehension experienced by many ESL and international students in public speaking classrooms. Honour offers strategies to help instructors adapt to teaching in a linguistically diverse classroom and to assist ESL students in overcoming their fear of speaking in front of others. These strategies include the use of an anonymous questionnaire to gain student feedback, the inclusion of issues of discrimination in classroom discussions, and short essays to encourage empathy among students. Honour emphasizes that all students should feel welcome and safe in the classroom environment and warns that avoidable missteps can inadvertently exacerbate the challenges faced by ESL and international students, leading to poor academic performance or excessive absences.

Howard, J. (Ed.). (2001). *Service-learning course design workbook.* Ann Arbor, MI: OCSL Press.

This workbook, a companion volume to the *Michigan Journal of Community Service Learning*, provides an extensive and helpful framework for self-guided service-learning course development. It is also useful for faculty development workshops. It covers conceptual frameworks, debunks common myths about service learning, and introduces the various components of academic service-learning courses. The section on principles of good practice covers a variety of key issues, such as establishing learning objectives, criteria for service sites, and preparing students to engage with the community. Emphasis is placed on development of appropriate academic learning objectives and the integration of civic learning objectives into courses across the disciplines. A variety of assessment methods, rubrics, and reflection activities are included, along with tips for community partnership development and maintenance. The bibliography includes resources for faculty as well as suggested readings on civic engagement for students.

Hugenberg, L. W. (1996). Introduction to cultural diversity in the basic course: Differing points of view. *Basic Communication Course Annual, 8,* 136–144.

The author posits that Americans tend to be insensitive to other ways of thinking, and that instructors of public speaking tend to resist change. Hugenberg offers strategies to overcome these basic challenges, such as having students develop speeches on a culture other than their own, and instructors developing assessment models that are more accommodating to individual and cultural differences. The author points out how difficult it is to design assignments that resist students' tendencies to stereotype; however, he positions the public speaking classroom as an ideal context for teaching students to listen to people from different cultures.

Koester, J., & Lustig, M. W. (1991). Communication curricula in the multicultural university. *Communication Education, 40,* 250–254.

The authors recommend that instructors adopt a multicultural perspective in their choice of curricular content so that students can develop ways of knowing that are generalizable beyond the dominant U.S. culture. Koester and Lustig stress that the public speaking classroom can advance communication theories, helping students structure messages, support ideas, and present research in ways that are not limited by Anglo cultural values of individuality and directness that may be appropriate only for members of a limited number of cultures. The authors recommend that orientation programs for international students include faculty who teach public speaking courses to encourage them to develop culturally diverse content and instructional approaches in the classroom and curriculum.

Levis, J. M., & Grant, L. (2003). Integrating pronunciation into ESL/EFL classrooms. *TESOL Journal, 12*(2), 13–19.

Intelligible pronunciation is a prerequisite to effective communication in the U.S. college classroom because words must be recognized by audiences if they are to process meaning. Most instructors receive little training in this skill and are unsure how to teach it in their public speaking classrooms. The authors outline challenges to teaching pronunciation and offer extensive strategies to help instructors gain awareness and effectively integrate this topic into their pedagogy through explicit instruction. Levis and Grant offer classroom activities related to word clarity, stress, rhythm, and intonation.

Meloni, C. F., & Thompson, S. E. (1980). Oral reports in the intermediate ESL classroom. *TESOL Quarterly, 14*(4), 503–510.

This article presents instructional materials for an intermediate level ESL course on public speaking. Meloni and Thompson offer advice for students who are choosing topics, reviewing recorded drafts of their presentations, and answering questions after their in-class delivery. The discussion of topic selection is particularly useful. The authors explain that assignments should be designed so that ESL and international students can establish credibility as speakers with an interesting background and knowledge expertise, rather than falling back on topics that reinforce overly simplified cultural stereotypes. The authors also provide assessment rubrics for instructors and for student peer feedback.

Mendoza, S. L. (2005). Bridging paradigms: How not to throw out the baby of collective representation with the functionalist bathwater in critical intercultural communication. *International and Intercultural Communication Annual, 28,* 237–245.

In this meta-theoretical article, the author encourages readers to embrace a more complex understanding of communication, identity, culture, and ethnicity, as opposed to one that is more reductive. She asks readers to consider the challenges international students face in terms of rigorous socialization. The author's insightful reflections on this seminal article are published separately in *The Handbook of Critical Intercultural Communication* (edited by Nakayama and Halualani in 2013). The *Handbook* and the journal in which this article appears are both excellent sources for considering the relationship between communication and culture across a variety of settings and for following the trajectory of cultural and intercultural communication theory and research.

Modaff, D. P. (2004). Native virtues: Traditional Sioux philosophy and the contemporary basic communication course. *Basic Communication Course Annual, 16,* 261–278.

The author examines the philosophy and practice of communication education as potentially transformative for students. Modaff explores ways that traditional Sioux virtues of bravery, generosity, fortitude, and wisdom can be incorporated into the teaching, evaluation, and interactions he has with his students in the public speaking course. The emphasis on learning objectives is shifted somewhat from individual achievement to community well-being. The article contains useful innovative practices and ideas for generating effective assignments.

Murphy, J. M. (1991). Oral communication in TESOL: Integrating speaking, listening, and pronunciation. *TESOL Quarterly, 25*(1), 51–75.

The author discusses the teaching of speaking, listening, and pronunciation skills as key features of a coherent curriculum design in the ESL classroom. Although Murphy argues for an integrated model for teaching these foundational skills, the section on pronunciation is particularly useful. The author points out that ESL students need additional practice with "less tightly controlled opportunities to express themselves fluently and spontaneously" if they are expected to increase their communication competence. Murphy offers an extensive list of classroom activities to teach oral communication that integrate opportunities for students to practice speaking, listening, and pronunciation skills.

Murphy, J. M. (1992). Preparing ESL students for the basic speech course: Approach, design and procedure. *English for Specific Purposes, 11*, 51–70.

The author describes a "discovery process" method for preparing ESL students to succeed in the public speaking course that emphasizes dyadic interaction and cooperative learning. Using this method, students are encouraged to work in small groups and practice delivery of presentations on a variety of topics and to hone their listening comprehension by practicing note-taking skills. He argues that the traditional public speaking assignment (i.e., individual students taking turns speaking to the whole class) should be de-emphasized in favor of dyadic interactions that build interpersonal communication skills and confidence. The author's discussion of instructional materials is particularly useful. Drawing on published literatures in process-based ESL teaching, Murphy offers detailed descriptions of classroom activities and assessment procedures aimed at measuring outcomes in this preparatory course he recommends be included in the college curriculum.

Murphy, J. M. (1993). An ESL oral communication lesson: One teacher's techniques and principles. *Basic Communication Course Manual, 5*, 157–181.

The author encourages instructors to reflect critically on their teaching methods and to offer ESL students authentic classroom experiences in which they can develop necessary skills that will help them thrive in U.S. higher education. The article includes detailed instructions to help students learn how to be competent speakers and listeners, as well as assessment forms to help instructors track learning. Murphy recommends that instructors maintain a "retrospective account" of each class session they teach. He offers a set of thirty such observations, each connected to teaching principles underpinning classroom activities. In this article, Murphy provides an important instructional alternative to traditional assignments and posits approaches to teaching public speaking in increasingly diverse classrooms.

O'Hara, J. B., & Leyva, A. (1996). Cultural diversity in the basic speech class: Disaster or opportunity? *The Florida Communication Journal, 24*(2), 90–101.

The authors review how different values among students in the public speaking classroom can impact learning objectives, assignments and activities, and interpersonal behaviors. Focusing on challenges faced by ESL and international students in introductory communication courses, O'Hara and Leyva identify common academic challenges, including taking written exams, understanding lectures, participating in group discussions, and delivering oral presentations. They point out that effective teaching depends on the instructor's "sensitivity to and skill in adapting to the particular needs and values of international and ethnically-different students." The authors' discussion focuses on issues of assessment of student work, facilitation of classroom interactions, and attitudes about silence and nonverbal transactions.

Quigley, B. L., Hendrix, K. G., & Freisem, K. (1998). Graduate teaching assistant training: Preparing instructors to assist ESL students in the introductory public speaking course. *Basic Communication Course Annual, 10*, 58–89.

The authors describe strategies for graduate teaching assistants assigned to public speaking courses with mixed populations of native English-speaking students and linguistically diverse students. The assessment of ESL students' speaking proficiency is prioritized as a necessary skill for graduate teaching assistants. The authors also emphasize the benefits of consulting with campus resources and making collaborative decisions in an effort to support ESL students and their varied needs. Using a rhetorical approach to instruction, the authors recommend assignments involving interviewing and research about U.S. culture as particularly helpful to integrate learned skills. This article includes an extensive reference list to guide readers to additional relevant sources.

Rubin, D. L., & Turk, D. (1997). The basic communication course: Options for accommodating non-native speakers of mainstream North American English. *Journal of the Association for Communication Administration, 2*, 140–148.

The authors provide strategies to help instructors of performance-based public speaking courses meet the needs of linguistically diverse students. Rubin and Turk explore several options, including developmental courses as prerequisites for public speaking, strategies to mainstream ESL students into conventional public speaking courses, creating special ESL sections of public speaking courses, and "culturally inclusive" sections of public speaking courses that integrate ESL and native English speakers.

Shih, R-C. (2010). Blended learning using video-based blogs: Public speaking for English as a second language students. *Australian Journal of Educational Technology, 26*(6), 883–897.

The author offers an approach to teaching public speaking for linguistically diverse students that includes online and face-to-face blogging in order to promote self-directed learning and increased levels of student satisfaction and motivation. Shih points out that blogging can offer an interesting way for ESL and international students to share their opinions, interact with others, and achieve educational learning goals. The students agreed that online settings provide a safe learning environment in which to practice skills and receive feedback from instructors and peers. In addition to gaining public speaking skills, students can also gain proficiencies in multimedia software.

Smallwood, B. A. (1976). Public speaking in the ESL classroom. *TESOL Newsletter, 10*, 9–10.

The author describes how citizens in Nigeria are often judged by their ability to speak English in public settings. Smallwood explains how one's credibility is determined by abilities associated with pronunciation, intonation, grammatical competence, and vocabulary control. In this very brief article, the author emphasizes that, in the public speaking classroom, it is important for ESL students to practice and gain confidence speaking about topics that have importance to the speaker and the audience in order to promote class cohesion and unity.

Yang, L. (2010). Doing a group presentation: Negotiations and challenges experienced by five Chinese ESL students of commerce at a Canadian university. *Language Teaching Research, 14*(2), 141–160.

The author describes challenges faced by Chinese ESL students preparing to deliver oral presentations at a Canadian university. The students utilized peer-to-peer dialogues and email exchanges to overcome their underdeveloped English conversational abilities as well as to clarify learning goals, generate topic ideas, and arrange practice rehearsals. Yang draws on language socialization theory to understand how the Chinese students overcame their lack of familiarity with the academic expectations or skill-based competencies regarding oral presentations, despite satisfying the typical admission requirements of North American universities (e.g., TOEFL scores). The author also discusses some of the challenges faced by ESL and international students who are assigned collaborative "group work" for the first time.

Yook, E. L. (1997). Culture shock in the basic communication course: A case study of Malaysian students. *Basic Communication Course Annual, 9*, 59–78.

The author describes how many ESL and international students fear appearing "foolish in front of peers and teachers, and feel stripped of their real selves and their real language capacities" in the public speaking classroom. Yook examines the case of students from Malaysia enrolled in public speaking courses in the United States who report experiencing "culture shock." The impact of culture shock on the Malaysian students manifested in tendencies such as avoiding eye contact with their peers and instructors, and other nonverbal behaviors that were perceived as counterproductive to the learning process. Yook provides a useful overview of cultural norms that, in combination with English language deficiencies, can negatively impact ESL students' success in the public speaking classroom. These communication norms are related to nationality, gender, religion, and social class. For example, in Malaysian culture, gesturing and talking loudly are seen as disrespectful, especially for female speakers. Yook offers suggestions for instructors that include the adjustment of expectations and modification of assessment criteria.

Yu-Chih, S. (2008). The toastmasters approach: An innovative way to teach public speaking to EFL learners in Taiwan. *Regional Language Centre Journal, 39*(1), 113–130.

The author describes a student-centered method of teaching public speaking to ESL and international students that focuses on building confidence, succeeding in academic settings, and preparing for speaking roles in professional contexts. The method proposed is part of a program offered by Toastmasters International, a nonprofit organization that teaches English-language public speaking in ninety countries. Yu-Chih implemented this method in a classroom in Taiwan and found students' responses generally favorable with regard to reduced anxiety, increased public speaking skills, and advanced English language proficiency.

Zappa-Hollman, S. (2007). Academic presentations across post-secondary contexts: The discourse socialization of non-native English speakers. *The Canadian Modern Language Review, 63*(4), 455–485.

The author describes challenges faced and the coping strategies implemented by graduate students from several countries of origin who were assigned the task of delivering an academic presentation at a Canadian university. The challenges faced involve linguistic (e.g., limited fluency), sociocultural (e.g., lack of understanding of academic norms), and psychological (e.g., shyness and fear) issues. In terms of the academic tasks, the students expressed particular concern about being assigned to talk extemporaneously and being expected to answer questions after a presentation in an open discussion period. Drawing on second-language socialization theory, Zappa-Hollman points out that in order to meet their academic goals, ESL and international students must possess sufficient language proficiency as well as a good understanding of the behaviors valued by the institutional context. In addition, many ESL students find it helpful when instructors model the activities assigned and explicitly communicate their expectations on assignments.

Zimmermann, S. (1995). Perceptions of intercultural communication competence and international student adaptation to an American campus. *Communication Education, 44,* 321–335.

The author describes factors corresponding to the academic success of international students studying on U.S. campuses. Zimmermann highlights the importance of international students' talking with American students and positions it as the most important factor in helping them adjust to American life and increasing their communication competency. The frequency of such interactions is a key indicator. International students who describe their college experiences as having little contact with native speakers report having the least amount of confidence in their oral English skills. Findings suggest that we should rethink policies that segregate non-native English speakers from native English speakers in our public speaking courses. Special sections deny international students important opportunities to interact with native English speakers and ignore the fact that native English speakers have much to learn from their international peers.

Index